RGSE

D1446189

carmen

"The PICU Baby"

A Journey of Medicine & Miracles

carmen

"The PICU Baby"

A Journey of Medicine & Miracles

SYDNEY N. HATCHER

INVICTUS MANEO PRESS

Centreville, VA

www.invictusmaneopress.com

Copyright © 2018 by Sydney N. Hatcher

All rights reserved under International and Pan-American Copyright Conventions. By payment of the required fees, you have been granted the nonexclusive, nontransferable right to access and read the text of this e-book on-screen. No part of this text may be reproduced, transmitted, downloaded, decompiled, reverse-engineered, or stored in or introduced into any information storage and retrieval system, in any form or by any means, whether electronic or mechanical, now known or hereafter invented, without the express written permission of Invictus Maneo Press.

Any Internet addresses (websites, blogs, etc.), authors, and thought-leaders referenced in this book are offered as a resource to the reader. They are not intended in any way to be or imply an endorsement on the part of the author or publisher, nor do they vouch for their content.

Names and events in this book have been used and referenced by permission.

ISBN 9781724973931

Unless otherwise marked, Scripture quotations are from The Holy Bible, New International Version®, NIV®. Copyright © 1973, 1978, 1984, 2011 by Biblica, Inc.® Used by permission of Zondervan. All rights reserved worldwide. www.Zondervan.com. The "NIV" and "New International Version" are trademarks registered in the United States Patent and Trademark Office by Biblica, Inc.®

To my daughter Holland,

Your joy is contagious.

You will not fully remember this season of life, but I will always remember the way you encouraged me to walk with overwhelming grace and hope no matter what.

Contents

Introduction

This is the story of my daughter Carmen, who lived in the Pediatric Intensive Care Unit at INOVA Children's Hospital. She was born at thirty-four weeks' gestation after a fairly normal pregnancy. Four days after birth, Carmen received the first of many diagnoses that changed our lives forever.

Every single day Carmen taught me to be strong and to find something to celebrate, even if I had to make it up myself.

Be strong. Be brave. Miracles exist.

This is Carmen's story, but it will always be my song.

Carmen's mommy,

Sydney Hatcher

November

OUR SAVING GRACE

November 24th, 2017

I so badly wanted to get the Christmas tree up. I know it's early, but I feel like it's now or never.

Since I am on bed rest, Nate did all the work. I had wanted a picture of my pregnant belly in front of the tree before our baby girl arrives. My due date is January 6th, but I don't think I am going to make it until then. This will have to suffice.

I stood up just long enough to have my picture taken and I am back down for the night. Sweet Dreams, little girly.

November 26th, 2017

Baby girl is really wanting to experience life on the outside.

My birth plan has changed drastically. I will no longer be able to deliver at the natural birth center because I am preterm. We hope to get the contractions under control and keep baby girl in for a few more weeks!

I have received steroid injections to help with little one's lungs in the event she does come early. I do not even know which doctor would deliver her here at this hospital.

P.S. Today is my 27th birthday!

November 27th, 2017

While yesterday was an interesting birthday, it was honestly far from bad.

I am blessed to be 27 years old with so much to be grateful for! Not only did I have a few visitors and eat some cake, but the Steelers won, I was able to watch the Miss Universe Pageant, and was even able to rest up a bit. Yay me!

Here's to 27! I'm ready for ya!

November 30th, 2017
10:51 AM

After almost two weeks of attempting to delay her birth, Carmen Grace Hatcher is now earth side. She is the biggest, little miracle we ever did see.

At just 3 pounds, 12 ounces, and 17 inches long, Carmen is tiny, but mighty!

Mommy, Daddy, and all of our family are overjoyed and shocked at how these last days have played out. We are looking forward to assisting baby Carmen as she grows into the perfect fourth member of our family. I only got to hold her long enough to have this photo taken.

She has been taken to the NICU for observation with Daddy close behind!

God showed us favor today. We thank each of you who have prayed for Carmen, the doctors, and her delivery into this world. We love you all.

Carmen Grace shares a birthday with her grandma, Grace, and grace is exactly what we have experienced!

December

A UNIQUE GIFT

December 1st, 2017

Carmen had a great first night in the NICU at INOVA Children's Hospital!

As much as my heart longs to have her close to me, God has prepared me for this season of separation. While we are unsure of when she will be discharged, we are confident she is exactly where she needs to be right now.

Mama got to hold her for two continuous hours this morning and today the nurses will begin to feed Carmen with my milk, which is awesome! I pray that she can tolerate eating so that central line access will not be necessary.

I have been sent home from the hospital already and am blessed to go home to see Holland tonight. I am so excited to prepare our home for Carmen's arrival whenever that will be.

Physically, I feel great — like I never even had a baby. It will be strange to leave the hospital without her but I have so much to do before she comes home. I am grateful for the opportunity to get everything in order before she joins us! I can't wait for Holland to meet her!!!

December 4th, 2017 (Morning)

If you'll be my hero, I'll be yours.

One day at a time sweet girl. We can do this!

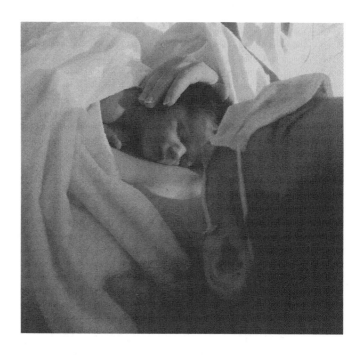

December 4th, 2017 (Afternoon)

Prayers are needed for Carmen today.

The doctors are planning to place a PICC line this afternoon. PICC is short for *Peripherally Inserted Central Catheter*. This will be a sterile procedure that will take an hour. If successful, it will allow Carmen to have more nutrition and it should stay in longer than the standard IVs she has been administered up to this point. The plan is also to place what is known as an NG tube, which is a feeding tube running through her nose to her stomach.

I will not be able to touch her for 24 hours after this procedure and an x-ray will be completed every 12 hours to make sure the NG tube and central line have correct placement.

Speech therapists have been contacted to come consult on Carmen's jaw. They believe it is recessed and a remedy may enable her to better coordinate the sucking motion.

Prayers are accepted for Mama, too. I know this is best for her, but it all looks very scary and it's hard for me to see. I got to snuggle her for 30 minutes today and, goodness, she is such a gift!

December 6th, 2017

To recap, on November 30th we welcomed our little miracle, six weeks early.

At just 3 pounds and 12 ounces, Carmen Grace Hatcher stole our hearts. Moments after birth, Carmen was taken to the NICU for observation and growth.

After two days in the NICU, it became necessary for Carmen to have a central line and NG tube to help her grow. She was slow to eat and the IVs were not holding. The central line could not be placed.

While being monitored, one of the doctors detected a heart murmur, while other doctors did not. At that time genetic counselors came in to see Carmen and noticed that her chin and jaw were unique. The doctors ordered an echocardiogram, which is a diagnostic cardiac ultrasound. A connection between these characteristics was suspected so genetic tests were ordered as well.

The echocardiogram revealed that Carmen has a heart defect that does not allow blood to flow from her heart to the rest of her body. Because she was born early a specific blood vessel called the *Patent Ductus Arteriosus*, open while she was in my womb, had not closed. As of today, after four attempts, a PICC line has been placed so that Carmen can receive medicine to keep this blood vessel open. The PICC line is also giving her all of her nutrients since she is unable to feed otherwise.

We were told that babies with this condition usually go undiagnosed until it is too late. We are thankful Carmen was born early, which led to her being under constant monitoring in the NICU. This led to a discovery that would have most likely been overlooked.

Within the next two weeks Carmen will have open-heart surgery.

These words are not easy to type, speak, or think, but I know she is strong.

This week has been heartbreaking, yet we remain faithful. We serve an amazing God and we are relying on Him more than ever.

December 7th, 2017 (Morning)

Happy "1 week," Carmen Grace!

You are the strongest person I have ever met!

This week has been the hardest week of my life and yet I can so clearly see God at work.

While I am still receiving more news on Carmen's health I know that, no matter what, she was born into the perfect family to love and care for her.

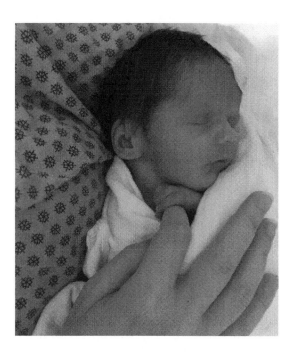

December 7th, 2017 (Evening)

We are...

December 8th, 2017

It has been so difficult to try to do life this week.

God has blessed me with Holland who has helped me find joy and hope when I struggle to see any. Holland will be the best big sister ever! I just know she will love and care for her baby sister! I can't wait for the day they can be together.

December 9th, 2017

Last night I decided to sleep in the NICU.

Although Carmen can't spend a lot of time out of her tiny home, I did manage to hold her for two hours. There is no other place I wanted to be. I got to pray for her and sing to her. I think she enjoyed it, too. I will treasure last night forever.

Today, Carmen is waiting on an MRI of her brain. She has a team of specialists lined up to examine her as we await genetic test results. The fear of the unknown creeps in. While it isn't finalized, we have been told that Carmen could have open-heart surgery as early as this Thursday.

I have web-searched every possible syndrome that Carmen could have and my head is throbbing. Over the last few days I have pled with God to take away certain diagnoses while at the same time trying to be realistic regarding the doctor's findings.

However, my prayer has changed. With God all things are possible and He wants us to come to Him for all things, both big and small. I believe in the miracles that Jesus has performed and I know healing Carmen completely is not too big of a prayer.

I am praying expectantly that God would heal her and that through this little life many would have their faith strengthened.

December 11th, 2017

The day after we received the news about Carmen's heart, we were told that she also has horseshoe kidney and *Cerebellum Hypoplasia*.

I was told to prepare to receive this kind of news every day.
I knew then that my prayer would be for Carmen's total healing! So many people have been praying in agreement. We thank you for your prayers and we feel them!

Yesterday, Carmen's MRI results came back and they did not find any further abnormalities in her brain. Praise God! The specific part which was labeled as underdeveloped is said to be small due to her gestational age and should continue to grow.

As for her kidneys, they are functioning fine and her specialist is not concerned with them at present.

Today, Carmen will have a sonogram on her spine because of concern with the tone in her lower body and a possible tethering. We also have two meetings, one with occupational therapy and one with physical therapy.

We have been blown away by the care Carmen has been given and we were thrilled to see her little home so nicely decorated. May God bless the hands that are helping her. She's a fighter!

December 12th, 2017

Today my mom and I met with seven of Carmen's doctors, nurses, and surgeons. We went into the meeting thinking that we would be receiving the detailed information on Carmen's open-heart surgery. However, that is not the information that was discussed.

Because of Carmen's size and the other health issues that have surfaced, there is a great chance that an open-heart procedure would be too difficult for Carmen to endure at this time. The surgery that she needs would be done in stages over the first few years of her life.

There is a possibility that a hybrid procedure performed in the next week could buy time for Carmen to eat and grow. This would entail the placing of a stint in the valve that is currently being kept open with medication, which would give Carmen a few months to gain weight and strength and recover at home as she awaits open-heart surgery.

This delay would also allow time for the genetic results and other findings to be put together and be better assessed.

A large team will be going over Carmen's case tomorrow evening. We will then have their decision on what they think is best in terms of the type and timing of the surgeries to be performed.

This was a difficult day as I am now realizing that Carmen will have multiple heart surgeries throughout the course of her life as opposed to a single fix-all procedure. Although it never seemed realistic to expect a quick fix for something so serious, I am now coming to grips with just how long this road will be.

There are milliseconds where the information is just too much and I feel like there is no way I can do this. Then I look at Carmen and realize she is the one fighting this battle and her strength fortifies me! God has created her perfectly and I know that He has sent this tiny angel to us for a reason.

December 13th, 2017

I wish I could write a better update right now, but things have changed yet again.

I guess we can just expect this to be our new normal.

On a positive note, Carmen's echocardiogram today showed that her heart might only require a remedy for what is known as an *Aortic Coarctation,* which is the narrowing of the large blood vessel branching off the heart delivering oxygen-rich blood to the body. She also requires a procedure to close one or two holes as well but this seems more manageable than reconstructive surgery to the entire left side of her heart.

Time will only tell how everything else will grow and what will need to be done.

Just as the meeting started, a nurse practitioner received news that the results from the genetic testing were in. They did confirm chromosomal abnormalities but they were unable to read exactly what that means for Carmen in the long run.

Tomorrow we will meet with a genetic counselor that will explain the results. The surgeon will also await these results before he decides on the surgery Carmen should have as well as the best timing. The specific genetic syndrome could effect how she would be able to recover.

As much as I feel numb right now, we are a day closer to answers. Nate got to hold Carmen for the first time tonight and even got to change her diaper.

In our eyes she is perfect.

December 16th, 2017

It's amazing what 24 hours can do, and even more amazing what 48 hours can do.

Two days ago I was so numb, so angry, so sad.

Just 48 hours ago we received the results from Carmen's genetic testing. We are still processing the information and are coming to terms with the fact that this will be a process every single day that involves making the conscious decision to choose the present over the future and joy instead of fear.

Carmen is **unique.**

In the best words that anyone can use, she is just that. A unique little girl who is perfect in her own way because she was "fearfully and wonderfully made (Psalm 139:14)." There isn't anyone quite like Carmen, just like there isn't anyone quite like you or me.

There is a map of maybes that suggest what life will be like for Carmen, but only she will determine which road she will take. Each day will have its own difficulties but each day is a gift.

She has already proven to be stronger than anyone believed and I will hold on to her strength and know that she can do anything!

As much as I want to look to the future, the fact is Carmen's heart surgery is the most important first step. We are still awaiting the exact day and time, and we ask that this first step be in your prayers over the next few days.

These last weeks we have been encouraged by so many who have been through similar situations and new relationships are blooming. There have been so many things that have happened that cannot be mere coincidence. We know God is at work!

Carmen is two weeks and two days old! Holland turned 22 months yesterday! Daddy's 30th birthday is tomorrow! We have SO much to celebrate and be thankful for!

Here is a little story that was sent our way. Obviously it was an eye-catcher for us because of our time spent in Holland, the impact that place had on us, and the fact that we named our first daughter, Holland.

Welcome to Holland

Written by:
Emily Perl Kingsley

"When you're going to have a baby, it's like planning a fabulous vacation trip—to Italy. You buy a bunch of guidebooks and make your wonderful plans. The Coliseum, the Michelangelo David, the gondolas in Venice. You may learn some handy phrases in Italian. It's all very exciting.

After months of eager anticipation, the day finally arrives. You pack your bags and off you go. Several hours later, the plane lands. The stewardess comes in and says, "Welcome to Holland."

"Holland?!" you say. "What do you mean, Holland?" I signed up for Italy! I'm supposed to be in Italy. All my life I've dreamed of going to Italy.

But there's been a change in the flight plan. They've landed in Holland and there you must stay.

The important thing is that they haven't taken you to some horrible, disgusting, filthy place full of pestilence, famine and disease. It's just a different place.

So you must go out and buy a new guidebook. And you must learn a whole new language. And you will meet a whole new group of people you would never have met.

It's just a different place. It's slower paced than Italy, less flashy than Italy. But after you've been there for a while and you catch your breath, you look around, and you begin to notice that Holland has windmills, Holland has tulips, Holland even has Rembrandts.

But everyone you know is busy coming and going from Italy, and they're all bragging about what a wonderful time they had there. And for the rest of your life you will say, "Yes, that's where I was supposed to go. That's what I had planned."

The pain of that will never, ever, go away, because the loss of that dream is a very significant loss.

But if you spend your life mourning the fact that you didn't get to Italy, you may never be free to enjoy the very special, the very lovely things about Holland."

December 18th, 2017

Today was a good day.

My mom and I got to spend the entire day with Carmen. Baby girl has been doing well with regulating her body temperature that she was moved to an open crib! It was so nice to see her out of that little plastic box habitat. Goodness, I was so proud!

Carmen had periods of time where she was very alert—the most alert I've ever seen her. My mom even read her a story, which was so sweet!

She has gained weight each day since birth and is now 4 pounds, 6 ounces! Yippee!

We met with the genetic counselors and surgeon once again to consult regarding her surgery.

Because Carmen is stable and growing, and because of the unknowns of Carmen's genetic differences, the doctors have decided it is best to wait a few weeks before her heart procedure. This would be close to Carmen's original due date.

Even though I am saddened because this means additional delays before she will be home, I think that this is the best decision for her in the long run. They want to give Carmen the best possible chance to be able to tolerate the procedure. If she could grow a bit, it is possible that this procedure could minimize or even eliminate the need for multiple surgeries throughout her childhood.

God's timing is perfect and today was indeed a good day.

December 20th, 2017

The last two days have been a bit worrisome as Carmen's PICC line ended up clotting and needed to be replaced.

Thankfully, as of an hour ago the new line is in, the old one is out and it only took two tries this time! The PICC line is how Carmen receives her nutrients and medication, so it's a big deal.

I got to see her right after the procedure and she was very alert again. As of today she is 4 pounds and 11 ounces! Even though I think she is now a big girl, my hand seems to dwarf her.

I am amazed by her strength! Even her nurse said she is a champ with needles, which certainly isn't something she received from me!

December 21st, 2017

Mommy & Carmen played dress up today.

Carmen's nurse got creative and made this single hat out of two. I don't have much of an update today and for that I am beyond grateful!

The cardiologists have approved that Carmen start drinking a bit more milk every four hours by mouth. I am ecstatic about this as it will hopefully lead to her coming home sooner post-surgery!

We are getting ready for Nate's parents, Gigi and Big Poppy, to come visit tonight.

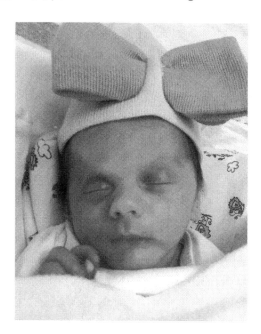

December 23rd, 2017

Today was a GIGANTIC day for Carmen!

Today she actually got a legit bath instead of a sponge bath! Aunt Lindsay was able to visit her for the first time and helped hold her tiny body in a bowl as I bathed her.

Carmen is now 5 pounds, 1 ounce of sweetness! We were able to adorn her with her Santa hat after she was squeaky clean. Thank you, Nancy, for this precious hat! You know I love accessories!

I am learning so much about choosing joy each day and focusing on the things that we so often take for granted. This could be a most difficult and dark season if I allow it to be. Instead, I will choose joy! I will celebrate the true meaning of Christmas and be thankful for each day. I will focus on the moments we have and THE ONE who gives them.

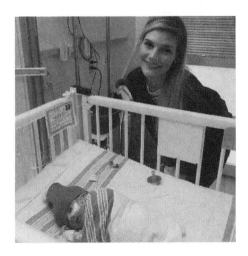

December 25th, 2017

Joy to the World!

Since Carmen can't wear clothes due to her lines, her nurse decided to put her in a stocking for a Christmas photo shoot today.

Goodness, she is just the sweetest!!

Lots of love has been packed into 24 hours. Merry Christmas from our family to yours!

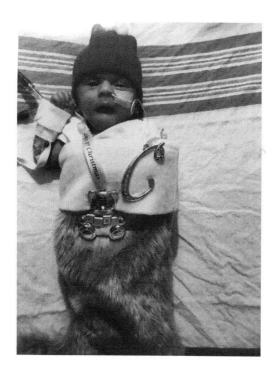

December 27th, 2017

You did it, sweetie!

Carmen, YOU are four weeks old!

I'm not exactly sure how that is possible, but it's true! A lifetime of love and heartache has been packed into these last four weeks, but you did it! Each day has challenges and I would have never thought I could have made it through all of this, but we did.

To think this is only the beginning is overwhelming at times. You, however, are my hero. You are SO strong and have made me stronger than I ever imagined! My faith has been strengthened and my love for God has grown immensely. I know He loves you more than I ever could, little Carmen!

Thank you for snuggling with me tonight and snoring loud, just like your daddy!

December 28th, 2017 (Morning)

This morning I woke up to a call that Carmen's third PICC line had clotted and access was getting slim for her to receive her heart medication and nutrients.

They have tried seven times in the last two days and had no success. I just got news that they attempted to place a PICC line in her scalp and in her neck that were both unsuccessful.

Carmen is now being transferred from the NICU (*Neonatal Intensive Care Unit*) to the PICU (*Pediatric Intensive Care Unit*) where they will decide what other procedures they can do to gain access.

I am praying for Carmen's strength and comfort through all of this, for the doctor's hands as they attempt to place these lines, and, if it's God's will, for complete healing.

December 28th, 2017 (Night)

Carmen's grandma, Grace, and I arrived to the PICU just as they finished Carmen's PICC line procedure.

They were able to get central access in her neck. Amen! It was a very stressful day for us all, mostly Carmen.

This evening Carmen began to *desaturate* (low blood oxygen concentration) more frequently and stopped breathing. This was a very scary moment for Grace and me. Thankfully the nurses were able to get to her in time and administer oxygen until she could breathe on her own again. The doctors did not find a reason for this but assumed that the stress of the day could have been just too much for her.

Carmen is in a big room with a big bed as she awaits her big surgery. Every day I am astounded how one tiny baby can endure so much. I was extremely hesitant to leave tonight but I know Carmen is in great hands. Our dear friend, Nancy, is on night shift and that is most comforting to me.

I got to pick out a pillowcase for Carmen's bed. This is one of the few decorations she can have near her. I chose a string-bikini-themed pillowcase because she has so many things attached to her. We can pretend they are strings on a bikini! Maybe tonight she will have sweet dreams of lying on the beach. One day you will feel the sweet sunshine, my love!

December 30th, 2017 (Morning)

I got to stay with baby girl last night in the PICU and we both at least got a little rest.

These days Carmen is working on feeding and trying to grow as much as possible before her surgery.

She has had a difficult few days and is usually exhausted but this morning Carmen was wide-eyed and ready for the day! My hope is that this week will be uneventful and that she will find peace and rest as we approach the targeted surgery date.

December 30th, 2017 (Evening)

Perhaps this is the moment for which we were created....

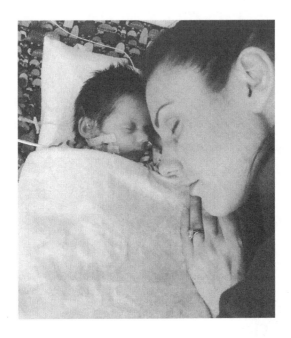

December 31st, 2017

We are closing out 2017 on the most positive note ever!
Our two baby girls got to meet for the first time today! Our family was united.

I am so grateful for this brief moment as it has been long-awaited and very desired. Thank you to the staff and child-life workers at INOVA for allowing us to bring Holland even though she isn't two yet. Thank you for allowing us to gather on a weekend so Nate could be with us as well, ensuring we were all comfortable and that Holland wasn't afraid.

I can't think of a better way to celebrate all that this year has encompassed and all that the New Year will bring!

January

A NEW HEART

January 1st, 2018

Happy New Year!

Because Carmen is not allowed to wear anything that is not considered "hospital grade" it was time to get creative!

Carmen is currently bringing in the New Year in her very own bikini made from a baby hat! Her very first outfit.

Thank you, Nancy! I know some people might question this, but I think it's awesome!

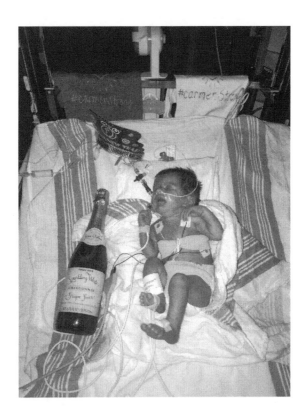

January 4th, 2018

Happy 5 weeks of life, Carmen!!!

Today was a monumental day for us. A date has been set for Carmen's heart surgery: Wednesday, January 10th.

Between now and then, Carmen will be given all that she can to grow bigger and stronger for surgery. My prayer for Carmen remains the same: **That she would be healed.**

January 6th, 2018

Happy DUE DATE, my love!

We are so blessed to have you in our family. We are also blessed to have been able to love on you with these extra six weeks you gave us! You are incredible! You have stretched my faith, my fears, and my heart.

I love you, Carmen Grace.

January 7th, 2018

Last night Carmen spiked a fever, so they had to culture her blood.

This morning the results revealed that she has an infection in her PICC line. The doctors have tried a few times to get a new line in, but to no avail. Another doctor will attempt a new placement and remove the infected one. If this cannot be done, they will have to work on clearing the infection from the current one.

This could impact the timing of Carmen's surgery. She is fighting really hard and her temperature has not come down. Her heart rate is very high and she is now on constant oxygen. It is very difficult to see her like this, but we have hope she will get through it all.

Thy will be done.

January 8th, 2018

Baby girl has had a great day today!

She looks 100% better than yesterday! Her oxygen saturation is great, she is off oxygen, and her temperature is down.

Unfortunately, Carmen got a staff infection and will have to wait until it is fully gone before she can go to surgery. It has been difficult to get so close and then start all over again. The hope is that Carmen can go into surgery in the best possible shape to give her the best chance of proper recovery.

God has been on the move and today has truly been another good day!

January 11th, 2018

Smile! You are six weeks old today!!!

Carmen is 5 pounds, 9 ounces and fighting with all her might. She is ferocious!

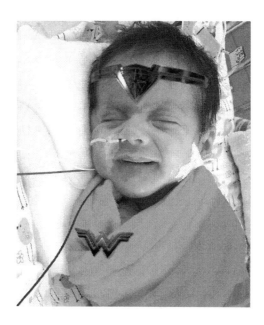

January 12th, 2018

Carmen has made her own rules from the beginning.

Her timing has been perfect and she has always been great at getting others' attention.

From the "beginning"...

When I was pregnant with Holland, my almost-2-year-old, I was absolutely terrified. I never knew I could or would have children. My health was certainly not the best when the pregnancy began and I didn't have the greatest access to healthcare. Nate and I were serving in a refugee camp in Montenegro for the entire year and I had been ill for months.

That spring, we had driven from Montenegro to the Netherlands, crossing seven borders, to attend a conference. The region (and former province) of Holland stole our hearts. It was exactly the renewal we needed after months of serving.

I found out I was expecting the very day we arrived back in Montenegro, which is how Holland got her name.

My prayer for Holland was that she would be healthy and would be a world-changer. I prayed that, unlike most of my life, she would have confidence and be strong. Today Holland is all of those things.

We spent the last part of our pregnancy back in Virginia and Holland was born February 15th, 2016. Nate and I brought Holland to Montenegro (that's not confusing) last May when she was 15 months old. We felt strongly that bringing Holland with us on a short-term mission trip would be beneficial to our family as well as the church we serve in Montenegro.

Before we began our travels I became anxious about bringing Holland with us. I asked God to direct me and clearly felt the Holy Spirit communicate to me, **"God will bless you for your faithfulness."**

I was filled with peace and I assumed this was the message to bring to the church in Montenegro. I did my best to encourage my brothers and sisters overseas to be faithful. I tried to remind those who previously had struggled how their lives had been transformed in real ways.

Halfway through the week, I knew I was pregnant. I took a test and laughed at the two lines that came up instantly. *Of course* we would find out yet again in Montenegro that we were expecting! God, you are so fun! Your timing is perfect!

I remembered the words, *"God will bless you for your faithfulness"* and thought, hmm… Could it be that Nate and I were being blessed with this pregnancy for our faithfulness? Awesome! Thank you, Lord!

My health was once again less-than-optimal, having been diagnosed with Hashimoto's disease (an autoimmune disease wreaking havoc on thyroid function), so the pregnancy was a miracle in itself.

I began my prayer for Carmen. I knew that Carmen would be the name if indeed we had another girl. I took Latin in school and in that language Carmen means "song or poem." My prayer for her was that *she would have a unique gift that would bring glory to God.*

I have to admit, I assumed maybe she would have a beautiful singing voice to worship with, or maybe she would be an excellent teacher but I didn't want to be too specific. I left it in God's hands.... *a unique gift....to bring Glory to God...*

Carmen Grace would be her name. That way both of our girls would have one of their grandmothers' first names for their middle names. The fact that Carmen Grace decided to be born six weeks early, on her Grandma Grace's Birthday, is still such a sweet gift to us all...and confirmation I picked the right name.

I pleaded to have a natural birth like I had with Holland, and even though Carmen was only three pounds, it was the most excruciating pain I've ever experienced. The second most painful was my appendix rupturing while pregnant with Carmen.

While in labor the doctors warned me that if Carmen's heart rate dropped again they would have to do an emergency C-section. It didn't. My water never broke and Carmen was born "en caul." I had read recently that being born "en caul"adds great protection to the baby. In history, being born this way meant the baby would be destined for greatness and would be protected. So far, I believe both of those to be true for little Carmen.

On day four of Carmen's life my world was turned upside down. I received seven phone calls in a row all from separate doctors, nurses, and specialists regarding Carmen's situation. One thing led to another and my heart was broken repeatedly.

First her jaw, then her kidneys, then her heart, then her brain. I was on the floor crying so hard I couldn't breath. It felt like someone had ripped out my stomach.

The worst part was, Holland began to fake cry next to me, unsure of what to do. I held her tighter than I ever had and realized in that moment just how wonderful of a blessing she truly is to me. I had taken her perfect health for granted and life as I knew it was changed forever.

Those next few days are a blur. Bad news continued coming in waves and I wondered when I would simply disintegrate. I assumed that's what happened to people who received this kind of news day after day. I thought I would just vaporize but, by God's grace, I didn't.

51

For two weeks we waited for the pieces of the puzzle to be connected.

When the genetic results came back we were told Carmen had significant genetic anomalies. Again, I assumed they would tell us the name of her syndrome and we would go from there. I didn't know that sometimes there's a first time for something.

I was handed a small packet of paper with the following on the title page: **Unique - Rare Disorders and Diseases.**

The genetic counselors spoke "*Carmen is... unique*, there isn't anyone quite like her, and we have no record of any other person having what she has."

My heart sunk. In this moment I had forgotten my prayer and I was in shock. How? Why? Is this a joke? Where do we go from here? How do we help her?

They gave me four short pages outlining a myriad of possibilities for her. I read that Carmen even being born was almost unheard of and that she may never walk, nor talk. I've been told she will have extreme delays in every sense and her health will forever be an issue. But I've also been told repeatedly that we just don't know. For now, I have immense hope in the unknown.

I still cannot answer any of these questions but I *do* know my prayer was answered.
Carmen has a unique gift that *will* bring glory to God!

With every passing day, Carmen is stronger than she should be. She has grown better than anyone expected, which has perplexed the professionals.

Tonight, after days of fighting a blood infection that delayed her heart surgery, we were told it is time. The valve that is being kept open with medicine to provide blood flow to her body has started to close. They have Carmen scheduled for heart surgery first thing Tuesday morning.

Carmen must stay well these next three days for her to go to surgery.

Before the doctor left the room this evening, she said, "I've been here for a long, long time. Have hope. You are allowed to have hope."

God's hand is at work. We have more than hope; we have His promises.

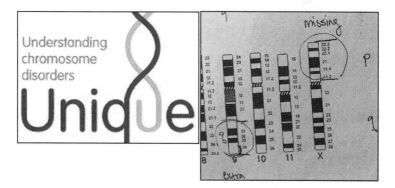

January 14th, 2018

This is real life. Genuine blood-sweat-and-tears, show-up-and-keep-pushing-forward life.

I never thought I would want to remember these moments so much, but I hope one day we can show Carmen these pictures to let her know just how far she has come. We are just two days away from heart surgery!

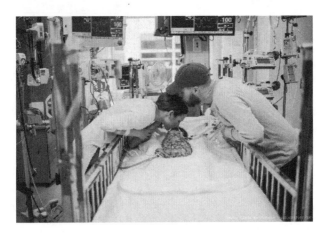

January 15th, 2018

I just got a call that, once again, Carmen has spiked a fever!

They are currently running tests. She is scheduled for surgery tomorrow morning but if anything comes back positive they will have to delay yet again. When I left the hospital a few hours ago she looked the best I have ever seen her!

January 16th, 2018

Open-heart surgery day...

Dr. C. just met with us and said that although it was a long and slow process, Carmen tolerated the surgery well. There were no surprises in the operating room and no surprises since she has been in recovery. She will be heavily monitored over the next few days.

The surgeons were able to enlarge her left vessel, which is the one responsible for pumping blood to her body. They closed the hole in the upper chamber of her heart and placed a PA (pulmonary artery) band in the lower ventricle to reduce blood flow to her lungs.

The goal is to have this configuration work sufficiently until Carmen is developed enough to have the septum between the lower chambers closed with a device. They are hoping that this band will allow her to grow for the next several months until she will be able to have the VSD (ventricular septal defect) closed. Her chest will remain open and covered with a sterile membrane for the next few days until the swelling goes down enough to allow closure.

We are still waiting to see our little warrior. Carmen is strong. God is stronger!

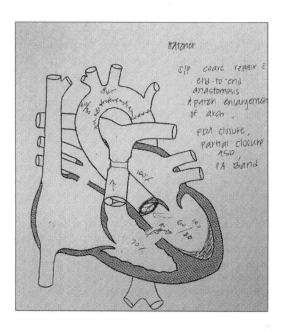

January 17th, 2018

I stayed the night with baby Carmen.

The last six weeks now seem like a lifetime as I look at her in her current state. It is as though every step forward opens a whole new staircase, but we will keep moving forward.

Throughout today Carmen will have more invasive procedures on her heart. After observing her overnight, some adjustments need to be made.

Given the complexity of her situation, she tolerated last night very well.

As a mom, seeing my baby in this condition has been a nightmare. Never in my wildest dreams would I think I could do this, but God is giving me strength to go on and fight right here beside her.

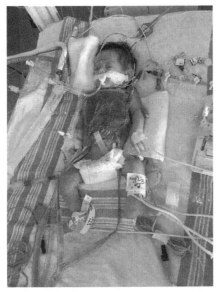

January 18th, 2018

The OR team is setting up in Carmen's room to go back in and tighten her PA band.

They could possibly remove the retractors today and begin a staged closing of her chest. Nate and I were unaware that they had to leave the retractors in her chest because of how swollen her heart was. I didn't even know that was possible. I am learning so much.

Just to be clear, this is written by a girl who passed out while getting her ears pierced. I really wasn't cut out to see things like this!

One day at a time. She really is my hero.

January 19th, 2018

I may regret sharing this, but this journey is bigger than just us.

Watching Carmen fight for her life in the hospital over the past seven weeks didn't prepare me for this week. Truthfully, it has been the hardest thing in the world just to look at my baby girl. No parent should ever have to go through this. Even though this surgery is a step forward, it has felt like falling back into those dark, negative places. I really can't explain it.

Carmen's surgery began Tuesday the 16th and every day she has had more procedures to tweak what was done. I wasn't prepared for such a lengthy process and it has been very discouraging. She still has quite a way to go before they will close her chest. And this will not be her last open-heart surgery.

For the last four days, I have had to look at a pile of lines, tape, and gauze on top of my beautiful baby as she has been medically paralyzed and constantly sedated. Even if I tried to close my eyes, the smell would overtake me. It is cold and sterile and feels downright torturous!

Yesterday, I sat in my car for twenty minutes attempting to get all of the tears out before walking in to see my baby. I then spent the next several hours back and forth hiding in the hospital bathroom in tears, knowing I have to pretend to be strong for her, my family, and even for myself. My stomach is churning.

This evening when I came in to see Carmen, I began to talk and sing to her. The nurses are weaning her off the medication that renders her paralyzed but she will remain very well sedated.

I kept talking to her and the nurses left the room. Moments later, Carmen's eyes, which have been half-open and dazed, locked contact with mine. Her lips and shoulder began to move slightly. I lost it.

The nurses came back in to see me frightened and in tears. I didn't know she was there, aware, and could hear me.

They assured me that this was a good thing and that she knew Mommy was with her. They asked if they could take a picture since she was staring right at me and I kept crying and said, "No." After I calmed down and thanked Carmen for letting me know she was OK, I asked the nurse to take a picture.

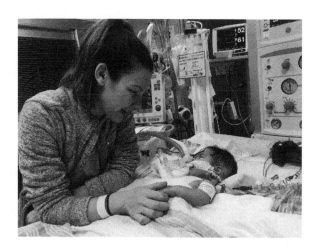

Having joined us on the journey through our story, I would ask you to consider doing something as a favor to me. Give your little one, no matter how big they are, a huge hug!

January 20th, 2018

Carmen's numbers have not looked well today and she will be receiving a blood transfusion soon.

January 21st, 2018

"God only gives you what you can handle."

This has been one of the notions I have embraced and tried to live by since my walk with Christ began. These words have comforted me in times when I thought my world was falling apart and when I needed to sort my mind as to what God would do next. I thought, "Surely He knows me best and will only give me what won't break me. It can get close, but He won't allow any more than I can endure."

Many people over my life have told me that my experiences (*especially* the trials) have made me strong. Sometimes the things I have faced after believing the above idea made sense. If I handled *that*, then God will let me go through *this*. Nothing more, because He won't give me more than I can handle.

This is the biggest lie I have believed as a Christian.

As I drive home tonight, it hit me. *I can't handle this!*

I can't handle seeing my baby like this. I can't handle all the information being thrown at me every day. I can't handle trying to be in two places at once. I can't handle or fathom what her (or my) future will be. I can't handle the thought of her not having a future at all. *I can't handle any of this!*

But He can.

He gives us far more than we can handle. If we could handle it on our own we wouldn't need Him. I thought I had prayed all that I could. I thought I had surrendered everything. I am pretty sure I even thought I knew Him as well as I could. I thought He had prepared me for this because surely He wouldn't give me more than I could handle. Surely He loves me so much that He wouldn't make me go through this. He must have picked the wrong "Sydney" in His book of names this time. Surely…

Actually, quite to the contrary! He picked the right one. He loves me more than I can begin to understand and He can handle all of this.

If you feel like you are unloved, like you keep getting slammed down again and again and you just can't handle it anymore… God loves you. He wants you to not only know Him but know Him intimately! He can handle all of it.

"Be still and know I am God." (Psalm 46:10)

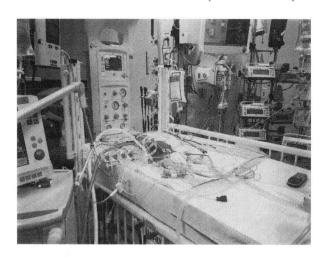

January 22nd, 2018

Carmen is about to have another procedure.

Within a few minutes the OR team will be prepping for the procedure to replace some of her central lines that have been in for a while and are no longer functioning at full capacity.

They will also explore her cardiac function, try and take out the retractors, and begin to close her sternum and chest if she tolerates it well. They anticipate her chest will need to be closed in stages with use of a wound VAC (vacuum-assisted closure) over a period of a few weeks.

January 24th, 2018

The OR team is coming up at 1:30 PM to work on retractor removal and chest closure.

Carmen has had retractors in her chest for eight days now. Despite all of this, Carmen is doing relatively well today.

January 25th, 2018 (Afternoon)

Carmen Grace is eight weeks old!!!

Lately, when people ask how Carmen is doing I don't know how to answer. But for someone considered by conventional medical science as *probably shouldn't have been born* I'd say she's doing great!

Carmen continues to be the strongest she can be! She is 6 pounds, 5 ounces and, my goodness, I can't wait for the day she can be in my arms again!

After being able to close her sternum yesterday, the doctors have begun weaning her off the ventilator starting today and have begun to feed her 1 ml/hour through her NG tube! Praise God!

The future for Carmen is still very unclear, and yet the future for each of us is as well. Every day is a blessing here on earth.

I am choosing to store up my treasures in heaven, that's for sure! My peace is in You, Lord, all the days of my life.

January 25th, 2018 (Night)

Big Poppy, Carmen's grandpa, came to visit and pray for Carmen this evening.

We also received tons of goodies from our church!

Our senior pastor and his wife visited us yesterday during Carmen's procedure. It was such a joy to have them with me in that moment.

We are so thankful for our church and all the support we have been given. We could not do this without you. Every day people see how you all have sacrificed for us and make our lives more manageable. I get to talk to people throughout the day about the amazing body of Christ and I am learning so much about helping others through your example!

I have had the honor of meeting other parents at the hospital and I have been able to give them some of your treats as well. Carmen is strong! And with all of you we are strong, too!

January 26th, 2018

Proud mama over here!

Carmen has been doing great! After a scare this morning that necessitated a new PICC line, Carmen seems to be going strong! The doctors have been weaning her off the ventilator all day and as of 8:30 PM she is doing mostly all the respiratory work herself. Depending on how she does tonight, they could extubate her tomorrow morning!

Slowly each tube and line will come out. One day at a time! We are cheering for you, baby girl!

January 27th, 2018

I get by with a LOT of help from my friends!

Today, two of my lifelong friends got to meet Carmen. This was such an important day for me because these two women have made me who I am today. They have been by my side since I was 11 years old! I know we will be best friends forever. I do not take this lightly because relationships are hard and life gets messy but through it all we remain.

Having Christie and Laura meet Carmen is something I will never forget. Friendships like these are rare and I know I will need these ladies as I walk this difficult journey. I am not alone.

January 28th, 2018

I am over-the-moon excited about this picture just received from my mom! She is visiting Carmen so I can spend some time with Holland.

Yesterday I was so disappointed to not be able to see my baby's face. She was so irritable and annoyed by all the tubes all over her, so to see her like this is a major blessing!

Carmen is coming off high doses of medication and has been experiencing withdrawal. Weaning will be a slow process with lots of changes happening over the next few days.

She is wide awake, taking breaths on her own, looking around and has even began to make cooing sounds! I have never heard her do that before! My heart is SO glad! I can't wait to go see her in a few hours. Yay, baby Carmen!

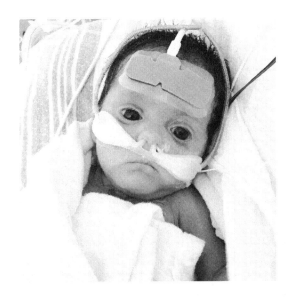

January 30th, 2018

I got to hold my baby!!!

Ugly crying took place, but after 15 days I got to hold Carmen!

It took some rearranging of the room and a bit of assistance but we snuggled for two whole hours!

Carmen has far fewer attachments. She is on high flow oxygen, TPN (total parenteral nutrition), pain medications, and a special formula to help her chest output. The rest of her medications are given orally as needed. The fact that I could list that is incredible because before today there would have been no chance I could have named everything!

From a cardiac standpoint, Carmen is exactly where she needs to be.

I truly wanted this to be a 100% good news entry, and honestly it is. But I do have a few prayer requests.
Carmen has begun making a few sounds and has a faint cry. She appears like she should be making more noise than she is. There is speculation that her vocal cords could have been paralyzed during her intubation. Tomorrow they will do a special test to see if there are any issues related to this.

Carmen is still experiencing withdrawal but she is significantly calmer today. Occupational therapy had their first meeting with her post surgery and they were thrilled to see her awake and content.

January 31st, 2018

Nine weeks ago I was given the green light that I could finally go into labor.

I was exhausted from weeks of trying to keep Carmen safely inside my womb, but one specialist decided that perhaps she was trying to tell us something. Indeed she was.

As much as we didn't know what she was trying to tell us, and as much as I was terrified and annoyed at how my delivery plan wasn't working the way I wanted, Carmen's birth was perfect. She was in control.

Ultimately, by being born early at the very hospital where she was delivered, she saved her own life.

Labor night was eventful as Nate, my mom, and my midwife tried to keep me calm and comfortable as we came up with a new birth plan.

I so desperately wanted a natural, non-medicated birth and, with their help, it was possible. Several nurses and staff members were curious if I would go through with it and one nurse asked if she could be present to witness the delivery because she never had seen anyone go "natural" with Pitocin. Since I knew there would already be an audience of intensive care nurses awaiting Carmen, what was a few more?

I think I attempted to break every hospital rule without putting Carmen in danger. I ate, I danced Tallava (a music and dance genre originating from Kosovo), I wore what I wanted, I pumped to stimulate contractions, took tons of homeopathies, bounced on my birth ball, and remembered I was made for this!

Thankfully, the doctor that delivered Carmen, who I had met just a few days' prior, granted all of my wishes. It took work, lots of help from my amazing husband, and a lot of confidence in my body, but we did it!

My beautiful angel will be nine weeks old tomorrow!

February

DO NOT LOSE HEART

February 1st, 2018

Mommy was super excited today and just had to celebrate the nine weeks of blood, sweat, and tears we had to wade through to get to where we are now!!!

Carmen, you continue to fight. You are a light and a force of hope! Thank you to all of her amazing nurses for helping me pull off a little photo shoot tonight!

You are the strongest bundle of pink anyone ever did see!

February 2nd, 2018

Another tube down! Carmen is now breathing all on her own.

She is almost to her first feeding goal through her NG tube.
TPN and lipids will be turned off tonight!

Transfer out of the ICU could be tomorrow!!!

February 3rd, 2018

Change of plans.

Carmen is still fighting withdrawal and has been very irritable again.

She did not sleep at all last night and her heart rate was almost 200. She is also running a slight fever.

They have decided to take a step back in her feeds from 14 ml/hour to 11 ml/hour and change some of her medications. The central line in her leg is slow to give any blood for labs, so a new line may be needed today.

Because of all of these changes Carmen will be staying in the ICU a bit longer.

Tonight I pray that Carmen can keep pushing through and even possibly let us know the direction to take.

February 4th, 2018 (Night)

It's after midnight....

Carmen has had a very eventful night; not in a good way.
Her oxygen saturation has dropped well below normal thresholds and she is really uncomfortable. Carmen has been very irritable but also equally exhausted, swinging from one extreme to the other. She is currently sound asleep.

At around 8:50 PM she aspirated her own vomit, so I rushed over and began to suction her mouth while calling for the nurse. It was the first time I hit the button on the wall and no one came for 11 minutes. I was able to clear her airway and administer her additional oxygen until someone arrived. This was very difficult because we cannot physically move Carmen's body since her sternum is still healing.

It was terrifying as Carmen went completely purple. After she came to, a discussion of what the culprit might be took place. We didn't know if it was a change of medication or a change in formula but Carmen is back on oxygen.

It was then discovered that her chest tube that is still draining fluid from her surgery had become disengaged. An X-ray was performed to determine if fluid is accumulating or air somehow got in when the chest tube came out.

February 4th, 2018 (Morning)

Yesterday I meant to share this picture of the shirt I ordered myself as a reminder of this journey. On it is written, "Daughter of the King."

My post was originally to be captioned: "I smile because I am His!"

The day didn't start off exactly as I had hoped. My morning call to her team wasn't the best and I was told we wouldn't be moving out of the PICU as planned. I swallowed my pride and my timing and decided to just have fun with Holland for the day. As much as I want to be with Carmen every moment, it is very unhealthy for me to be at the hospital 24-7.

As the hours passed I started getting anxious and eventually made it to the hospital at 5 PM. Things were not good. Around 9 PM I thought I was losing my baby. By 1 AM I was exhausted and defeated. I kept looking at my shirt and reminding myself that Carmen and I are a lot alike. We both have a Father in heaven who loves us unconditionally.

I had cried about 17 times before deciding I needed to leave the hospital. I've been told that babies can feel their mother's emotions. For me, I feel that if I am not strong in that room, I should not be in that room.

It was a difficult choice to leave because Carmen was not doing well and I honestly didn't have much faith in what the rest of the night would be like for her.

I got in my car and headed home, crying and praying the entire way. I began screaming out to God, "If you are who you say you are, why won't you heal her? Do you hear us? Why is there so much pain? Where will your glory be shown? Why are you silent now? Why?!?"

I know the answer to all of these questions, and God knows I do, too.

So I got home and looked down at my now tear-stained shirt and really nothing had changed. He is my Father, the Maker of the universe, and the way, the truth, the life (John 14:6).

I will smile, because I am His.

February 6th, 2018

Carmen has had a rough few days.

While she is becoming more stable, she is certainly keeping us all on our toes.

Carmen's surgery was not a perfect fix. We knew going into this that she would still have to go through another heart surgery once she got big enough to tolerate it. The surgery that was performed still leaves a lot of variables for Carmen.
Bottom line is, Carmen needs to grow.

For much of Carmen's life she has been fed through her veins and has only recently been put on a special formula. Carmen has a blood clot in her chest and both her lungs and chest have fluid and air pockets making it harder for her to breathe and grow.

This Thursday she will be 10 weeks old and as of today she is 5 pounds, 9 ounces.

I have been encouraging myself to find at least one positive thing in each day and today was not an exception.

Most of the time when I come to see Carmen she is either sedated, experiencing withdrawal, or sleeping. Most days seeing her eyes is a treat.

I was given a set of little cards from one of her therapists to see if she can focus on things. Over the last several days I have been occasionally using a card featuring a snowflake and today she found it time and time again!

This might seem like such a small thing, but I have learned to celebrate and be thankful for these tiny victories!

February 8th, 2018

Today I packed up a bunch of adorable props and a special blanket to bring to the hospital for Carmen.

I even made a sign for her because it's time to celebrate TEN weeks of life! Sure, her life looks a vastly different than those of others, but it is her life, nonetheless.

I have been aiming to do a little photo shoot every Thursday to document her progress.

However, those pictures will have to wait because Carmen is not well. She needed another blood transfusion this morning, has vomited multiple times, has a temperature, diarrhea, and has been shaking for hours with an elevated heart rate.

She is being treated for reflux and what is possibly more withdrawal. The cause for all of this is still a mystery.

We have tried everything to attempt to give her just a bit of comfort. We even put her in her vibrating bouncy seat for the first time ever! I may have shed a tear or two because, even though today was awful, this is the first time Carmen has been in anything other than a hospital bed her whole life.

She only lasted a few minutes before we had to take her out again. So this week Carmen didn't get a cute picture. Not much about Carmen's life is considered "cute," but I really try to capture everything. I know she will want to see the pictures one day. I will want her to see how far we came and how hard she battled.

February 9th, 2018

It is with a numb yet peaceful heart that I write this.

Carmen is not progressing as well as she should. She is still vomiting, desaturating, and has a fever of 102. She will have yet another blood transfusion today and they have begun ordering numerous tests to get more information about her upper GI tract.

The decision has been made to send Carmen to the cardiac catheterization lab on Monday to precisely determine the pressure in and out of her heart and to her lungs. The cardiologist, Dr. T., who will be performing these tests is the same one who would be performing the second heart surgery Carmen will need.

It was originally anticipated that Carmen would need this surgery somewhere around her first birthday but now they have reason to believe that Carmen may need this surgery right away.

On Wednesday evening they will present the findings of all the tests and create a new plan.

It's as if I am experiencing horrifying déjà vu to think I will have to see my baby girl in that state again so soon but I also know that something needs to change and Carmen will have no chance at coming home unless we try.

A decision has not been made and we know that Carmen does things her way. I will try to keep my timeline out of this.

The doctors said Carmen is tough. She has proven herself strong and worthy of being given the best shot!

February 10th, 2018

A ship is always safe on the shore, they say, but that's not what it is built for.

February 12th, 2018 (Morning)

This week has been difficult and has taken a toll on my whole family. I wish I had the strength to go into some of the details but the challenge to acknowledge our failures can be daunting. I, like everyone, can only endure so much before I just can't anymore. It is my goal each day to humbly submit to God's sculpting hand, but sometimes that submission happens as I am unconscious on the hospital floor.

Situated in the midst of this rough week is a big day. Carmen will be going to the catheterization lab around noon. There she will be tested for heart flow and pressures and information will be gathered to determine when to schedule her next cardiac surgery.

This is a major procedure requiring that she be intubated yet again and put under general anesthesia. Intubation has been very difficult for her in the past. Her central line will also be removed and a new line will be placed. Nothing is done without risk.

February 12th, 2018 (Afternoon)

Getting ready to head down to the catheterization lab. I pray today will be a day of answers. God, please bless Carmen and all those giving her the best chance at a beautiful life!

February 12th, 2018 (Evening)

It has been decided that Carmen will have her second open-heart surgery tomorrow at 9 AM. God is within her. She will NOT fail!

February 13th, 2018

Surgery is finished.

The pulmonary artery band has been removed and a device is now closing the VSD. She did not have to go on bypass. They are closing her up now and Dr. T. said her oxygen saturation is at 100%! It will still be a while before she is up and we can see her.

Tonight she will be somewhat fragile but it seems like everything went smoothly.

February 14th, 2018

Valentine's Day has a very special place in my heart.

I began labor with Holland on that day in 2016, which means I will have a two-year old tomorrow!

Holland made a special card for Carmen today that I got to bring to the hospital in her absence.

As for my youngest Valentine…

Carmen has been able to make eye contact with me today and under all of this "stuff" she is battling like a little princess warrior.

She is experiencing the rare condition known as *chylothorax* (the leaking of lymphatic fluid into the space between the lung and chest wall), which is a major issue and a decision on how to stop the fluid draining will need to be made soon.

IV access is again very limited and a new line will need to be placed. Baby girl has a few more hurdles to jump through before we can move on to the BIG stuff such as eating and growing. Though she is little, she is fierce and it is time.

Carmen will be 11 weeks tomorrow and weighs barely six pounds.

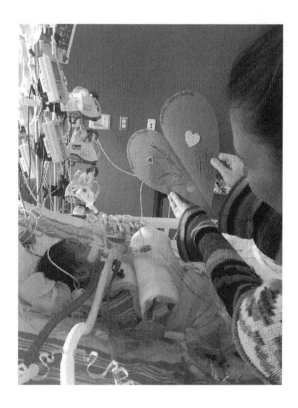

February 15th, 2018

Tomorrow morning Carmen is scheduled for interventional radiology at which time they will use picture guidance to place a central line.

From there she will most likely go straight to the operating room where they will perform another surgery to tie off the area from where fluid is draining. This is called a *thoracic duct ligation*. This has been an issue from her first surgery and they have finally come to a decision on how to approach it.

Another major event featuring a long day of waiting is upon us.

"Delight in the Lord, and He will give you the desires of your heart." (Psalm 37:4)

This verse has been heavy on my heart the last few days. I feel like I am clenching my teeth as I watch and plead with God to exert favor over Carmen. I rest in the fact that God loves her more than I ever could and I am doing my best to align my thinking and feelings with that fact.

My prayer for myself and my family and friends is that we would delight in Him so completely that we would smile at the hard days ahead and rejoice in the unknown. God is good even when things aren't!

Today was Holland's second birthday.

I woke up almost unable to move. I am not sleeping well and when I do I must be straining my whole body. There's a crick in my neck and everything hurts. God is good, though, and we were encouraged to spend some quality time with the birthday girl.

We made Holland a special breakfast, got her some cute new clothes and books and took her to an indoor play place. It was perfect because we were the only ones there! Holland, just like Nate and me, must sacrifice being exposed to large groups of people, especially children. With cold season at its peak, we have to be extra careful to avoid contracting something that could be fatal to Carmen.

Holland had a blast and I love spending time with her. She is going to be such a great big sister!

February 16th, 2018

Today is a good day.

I woke up early enough to not sit in traffic and made it to the hospital in time to have quiet moments with Carmen before the world awoke.

Today is a good day.

Carmen's eyes were open and so was my heart. I got to sing to her and pray over her before she was whisked away in her metallic medicine-mobile on her way to getting better.
One step toward bringing her home!

Today was a good day.

She came back from her first procedure with nurses that were upbeat and had a plan geared towards Carmen Grace Hatcher's recovery. We placed a tiny pink bow on her beautiful little head and seven people in the room agreed that today is indeed going to be a good day.

This I already knew.

You see, last night I had a dream about Carmen's funeral. I saw that through Carmen's life many would come to know Jesus Christ as Savior AND be baptized as a public profession of their genuine trust in Him. It was a beautiful vision to see.

When I was 21 and made the decision to follow Christ and be baptized I knew it would be a life-changing decision. And indeed it was. Every day that I wake up — even the bad days — are good. And the unknown days are known. And the daily circumstances do not change my future at all. I am secure.

See, even if the "worst thing" happened, nothing would change.

This life is fleeting; these good and bad days are numbered for us all. As I sit here watching my daughter squirming uncomfortably with a large needle in her side and covered in wires and tubes, I smile. Why? It's because God has favor over her. Best or worst case, His love remains.

There have been days where I giddily organize Carmen's room for her arrival, and others where I select songs for her funeral.

See, the decision I made to answer His call to follow Jesus, to marry a man of God who would help me raise our children in love and truth, and to love God abundantly more than anyone and everything else was the most important decision I could have ever made.

I have eternal life where every day is a good day.

"Therefore we do not lose heart. Though outwardly we are wasting away, yet inwardly we are being renewed day by day. For our light and momentary troubles are achieving for us an eternal glory that far outweighs them all. So we fix our eyes not on what is seen, but on what is unseen, since what is seen is temporary, but what is unseen is eternal." (2 Corinthians 4:16-18)

February 17th, 2018

This is the view from Carmen's window.

I am always adding and changing her room.
Sometimes the nurses come in just to see what is
on display day-to-day.

Thank you to those of you who have added to
the beauty of her journey through signs and
posters cheering her on! It may seem minuscule
but this colorful wall is a ray of light in what is
often a dark place.

February 18th, 2018

We have a specific prayer request for Carmen today regarding her chylothorax.

This morning Carmen's doctors performed a procedure to purposely create inflammation in her chest. This is done to help the lungs attach to the chest wall in hopes of sealing the space that allows fluid to accumulate. This is the second time this has been done this week. Depending on the outcome, they will decide if Carmen will need to go to surgery tomorrow. The surgery would be for ligation of the thoracic duct.

Carmen has developed a new heart rhythm during all of this that is of concern and her heart rate has once again become elevated. Our hope is that the rhythm was brought on by the stress related to these procedures and that it is only temporary. We pray for a successful procedure today and that she will not have to undergo another surgery tomorrow.

Until these issues are resolved, Carmen cannot be extubated or fed, among many other things.

She is getting a blood transfusion right now and is on several medications and supplements to keep her more stable as they figure out the cause and best plan of treatment.

Jesus, Carmen needs you!

February 19th, 2018

Inhale....

This is the face of strength. This is the face of innocence. This is the face of exhaustion, hunger, and bliss.

This is the face of patience and the face of incredible odds defied. This is the face of God's perfect creation. This is the face of my hero.

At just 11 weeks old, Carmen Grace has overcome three major surgeries, had numerous procedures, three MRI's, five blood transfusions, more than 100 X-rays, more arterial lines, mid lines, and central lines than one could count. She's had chest tubes, wires, breathing tubes, ports, suctions, and 900+ doses of medication — many of which flow constantly.

She's been paralyzed and sedated for most of her life and has only once consumed actual milk from a bottle.

She has a partially reconstructed heart that includes a device, and as of today a new set of titanium bands in her right side. She's had her sternum broken twice and her ribs stretched once. She's laid open with retractors in her chest for nine days! She's been poked and moved and in pain more than most people could possibly bear.

We now know that the chance Carmen had of being born alive were somewhere around 0.06%; and that's before all of her surgeries and complications.

Today I have what feels like a BURST of energy! Because, yet again, she is here! She is alive! God is SO GOOD!

He is teaching us patience and the importance of trusting Him every single hour.
When I look at Carmen I envision me holding her, and behind me I see all the nurses and doctors who have been here day and night fighting for her. And behind them I see each of you! All of our family, friends, and strangers who have truly carried us through this battle!

This is the face of community. This is the face of love.
This is the face of bravery. This is the face of us all. This is the face of a miracle.

Exhale...

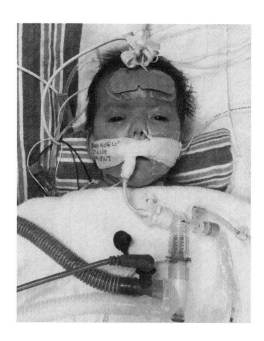

February 20th, 2018

Carmen got her breathing tube out today!

She is breathing almost completely on her own and receiving pressure to help open her lungs. This was a huge step!

Today I was reminded yet again that Carmen's surgeries will not be deemed truly "successful" until Carmen can breathe on her own, tolerate feeds in one way or another, and actually gain weight. This will be a very slow process but these are great things we can be praying about and these milestones are ones I look forward to meeting.

One big milestone is that Carmen would tolerate being held. I am desperate for this to happen soon, as it has been about three weeks since I was last able to hold her.

In the next few days, the doctors will be creating a nutrition plan for Carmen. They will eventually have to decide how Carmen should receive her feeds, whether it is by NG-tube, ND-tube or G-tube.

A big challenge for Carmen is to be weaned off all the heavy medications she has been receiving. The weaning process for Carmen will take several months.

Carmen is currently in her bouncy seat! They are using this as a way to distract her from the crazy tube she wants to pull off her face. Poor baby, I can't wait to see your face again!

February 21st, 2018 (Morning)

Carmen is not doing well.

She is going to the OR now. She is having extreme difficulty breathing. Mommy is on her way so stay strong, baby girl!

February 21st, 2018 (Afternoon)

Somehow, Carmen just avoided a *tracheostomy*, which is an opening surgically created through the neck into the trachea to allow direct access for a breathing tube.

When I arrived to the PICU, Carmen's nurse practitioner, Lauren, said she took a picture of Carmen before she went down to the OR in the event that Carmen returned with a trach installed.

My whole body hurts.

February 22nd, 2018

Today Carmen is TWELVE WEEKS OLD!!!

Miraculously, Carmen is coming in at seven pounds! No one knows exactly how that's possible, but she is!

Carmen is having a better day. No matter what, we will celebrate. What better day than today to have a good day?
Never would we have guessed that twelve weeks could be spent this way. Never could we have imagined the brokenness we would experience in this time.

So, today we celebrate. And Carmen and I invite you to celebrate this evening in a way that we cannot.

We ask that you hold one another. Hug one another. Kiss one another. Share your time with one another. Celebrate today. It's a good day.

February 26th, 2018

I guess it was bound to happen; I am sick.

Because of this I could not visit Carmen today. Thankfully Nate and Mimi got to see her. Nate even got to pick her up for a bit and I was told that she did great!

Carmen's breathing tube was taken out at around 9:15 AM and so far she is stable. Her oxygen saturation dips into the 70s when she is irritated but she has been recovering nicely.

With all of the other procedures, I forgot about one BIG step. Carmen's stitches were removed from her chest today!!! Thanks to technology, I got to watch them being removed via FaceTime. It was incredible!

We pray that Carmen will have enough strength to get through these next few days of breathing with step-down equipment and that she will soon be breathing completely on her own!

February 28th, 2018

Super Carmen!!!

While the road is long, Carmen is flying high and battling through each day just like the tiny superhero she is. After 26 days, I got to hold my baby today! I even feel like she has grown a bit. Tomorrow she will be 13 weeks and is staying at around the seven-pound mark. Today we commented that she now looks more like a baby than a preemie.

Currently she is fighting the mysterious onset of fevers, has *tachycardia* (abnormally fast heart rate) and has had some vomiting as well as other occasional drug withdrawal symptoms. She is enjoying the high flow oxygen rather than the huge oxygen mask that she fought for days.

In other news, Carmen received this super-amazingly-fabulous cape from the organization Tiny Superheroes, and it's just perfect! Thanks to whoever nominated her!

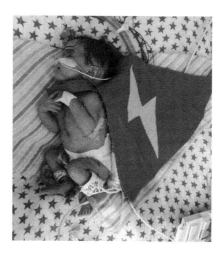

March

Luck Had Nothing To Do With It

March 1st, 2018

I don't want to forget that feeling of nothing —
where life was sucked from my limbs, eyes, and
ears until all that was left was my beating heart.

I don't want to forget that moment of despair —
when giving up and pushing forward seemed
equally as difficult and I stood lost somewhere
in between.

I don't want to forget the anger at myself, my
weaknesses, and even my God (the great I AM)
for not granting me my temporary wishes.

I don't want to forget that feeling of settling,
swallowing my pride, swallowing my tears,
releasing my dreams, hopes, and desires… to
Him. Not because it was *my* choice, but because
it was the *only* choice.

I don't want to forget the nights I awoke covered
in sweat, looking for my baby and rehearsed the
speech I had in my mind, reminding myself that
my current situation is in fact reality and not just
a passing nightmare.

The list goes on but, most importantly, I don't
want to forget how to retain this hope. This
great, unshakable hope that lies in Christ. The
hope that doesn't even promise the next earthly
moment, but promises even *more*.

More of something we can't even understand.
Something we could never imagine because we
have never seen or held it in our hands,
because… we settle. We fear. We forget. We
think we know what we want, what we deserve.

Oh Lord, my precious baby — the child you entrusted to me — has driven me to my knees and caused me to question every ounce of me and every ounce of You. I have repented for sins, even those I haven't committed, thinking it could change my present; maybe it could change her future.

I thought she was broken. I thought she was my punishment. I thought she was just part of the darkness that this world holds.

And she is. But she is so much *more*.

She *is* more of something yet I can't fully comprehend it! Something I couldn't imagine because I had never seen her, never held anything like her in my hands, and so… I settled. I feared. I forgot. I thought I knew what I wanted and what I deserved.

But she is *more*. She is exactly what I prayed for. She is exactly what my family needed. She is more than I ever deserved.

She has taught me to be brave. She has taught me what boldness truly is and how to walk in it.

Carmen has taught me to surrender, to be a servant, to be patient, to look for You in all places. She has taught me to have Your eyes. She has taught me to fight. She has taught me to love her, myself, others, and You. Yes, she has taught me to love relentlessly!

March 2nd, 2018

Triple yay and hip hip hooray!!!!

Holland got to visit Carmen tonight! It has been two months since she first met her. Their original meeting was only two minutes long. Carmen and Holland both did so well! I loved every moment of this perfect gift!

March 5th, 2018

Today at 3pm Carmen will have an upper GI test.

This is a test to gauge the severity of Carmen's reflux.

Her primary doctors have already talked to a surgeon about the installation of a G-tube, which is a feeding tube surgically placed in the stomach.

They will have to wait a few days for access to all the data from the testing once she is up to full feeds. For Carmen, a full feed would be 20 ml/hour. She will have to accomplish this before the surgeon will even consider a G-tube placement. Carmen is currently at 9 ml/hour.

We are a bit anxious about this and have suggested the possibility of waiting on yet another surgery. We will have more information later and decide what will be in her best interest.

As of today, Carmen is off all oxygen support! Her heart rate is still a bit high but otherwise she is doing well. Nate is at the hospital now and I will get to see her this evening.

March 6th, 2018 (Morning)

Carmen has had a wonderful WEEK!

Today she has been so aware, so focused, and… (wait for it)…she has a voice! I have never been so happy to hear my baby let out a big, loud cry! It was the first time she has truly cried! And it was beautiful! Of course, it wasn't all crying today, so below is a smiley picture after she got a bath and new bedding.

Counting it ALL joy!

March 6th, 2018 (Evening)

She's wearing a tutu! Yes, a TUTU!

Today after 14 weeks of life, Carmen was allowed to get dressed!

It took a lot of assistance to get her arms through her shirt because she is still very protective of her sternum, but we did it!

I think she is most beautiful!

March 8th, 2018

Today is International Woman's Day!

I want to take a minute to share about some incredible women I have gotten to know the last few months, and others whom I've known for a lifetime!

First, I want to give a huge shout-out to The Nest at Centreville Baptist Church. This is one of those "moms groups" hosted at my home church.

About two years ago a good friend of mine convinced me to try out a moms group. I wanted so badly to laugh because I knew for *certain* I wasn't a "moms group" kind of mom. However, over the last two years I have experienced a tremendous amount of love, learning, and support, which includes praying for one another. I have loved getting to know the various faces of "mom" and the many unique qualities that other moms have. It's just beautiful how life molds people and how God uses us to bless one another!

Next, I want to thank my friend Bella for being a solid rock-of-a-person. She is exactly the kind of woman I hope to become. She is strong and consistent and has helped me more than I could ever put into words.

Kristen D., while we have yet to meet, you made those early weeks so much easier because you had been in similar trenches. You made every little detail of what my life was like a little easier. You allowed me to see beauty in that hospital room and you have taught me how to be a light to strangers.

To my dearest friends Christie, Laura, Crystal, Susan, Ciara, Alyssa, Masha, and Janelle: thank you each for your encouragement, for checking in on me, for not only accepting me but also challenging me. I look up to you all so much! Each of you has helped me in so many different ways. You have made me a better person and have really impacted my entire family.

Some of these women have watched Holland while I was in the hospital and some have sent things halfway across the world just to make me smile. One sat with me in the hospital while I was in labor while she was also very pregnant, and one came to see Carmen when it was still difficult even for me to get to see her.

To Nancy, from the beginning you have been there to help me understand words, concepts, and learn how to be the best mom I could be in this situation. You have cried with me and reassured me. You have been an angel to Carmen and I know, without a doubt, that God arranged her to be in your care for a very special reason.

To Mimi and Gigi, I can't begin to thank you both for all the hours you have put into making this work. You have given Holland stability, confidence, and the sort of love in this season that I could not provide. Both of you have sacrificed your own families, your own free time, even your jobs, for us. We are truly thankful. You have each been vital in making sure I spend needed time with Carmen and have helped me to embrace whatever life will be like with her.

To the women who have sent cards, gift baskets, books, and meals, you have helped us maintain our sanity. You have made it possible for me to be a mom in two places and to even have little surprises for Holland! You have helped me to stay positive on the horrible days. You have given me the means to celebrate the good days and every second in between.

And lastly, I want to thank the nurses at Inova Children's Hospital. In the last 98 days, Carmen has been cared for by so many incredible nurses. In this time, I have made friendships and we certainly have our favorite nurses! I am constantly blown away by the outpouring of care.

Following is just a glimpse:

Nurse K. is such a light! Every morning when I call the unit, she answers with "Hi, mom!" The other day she helped me bathe and dress Carmen for the first time. She then moved a recliner from the other side of the unit into our room so I could hold her for hours comfortably. After this, she took pictures and told every nurse on the unit to come visit.

Last night when I arrived, K. was done with her shift and had not had Carmen as a patient. She came to see how we were doing and was immediately shocked that Carmen didn't have new linens and a new blanket. She quickly went and gathered everything to give her a bath, changed all of her linens, helped me get her dressed again, and put her gently in my arms. She made sure that Carmen was in perfect condition before she left. She stayed almost two full hours after her shift had ended to work with a baby who wasn't even her patient that day!

I will never forget all that these wonderful nurses have taught me! They have time and time again saved Carmen's life and mine!

There are truly hundreds of people I am not able to mention at this moment because my brain hurts but please know that every prayer, every note, everything you all have done for us has been more than we could ever deserve. May God bless you ALL for your faithfulness!

March 11th, 2018

Carmen came into this world 101 days ago.

She was tiny, but perfect. In my young mother's eyes she was beautiful. She was pure. She was innocent. She had everything working for her. She was brand new and unblemished.

On day four, my view of Carmen was tainted. "Bad news" changed my mind and this tiny little girl was now covered in marks. She carried baggage, she was needy, she was lacking, she was imperfect.

I told myself over and over again that she is created by a Maker who makes no mistakes; that in her own way she is perfect. Yes, in her own way she is perfect.

I told myself that she is in the perfect place at the perfect time to receive the perfect care she needs. Some days I convinced myself that Carmen would be fully recovered, fully fixed—just plain perfect—before she would journey home.

Tonight after a week of waiting, I felt God tell me, "Sydney, you will continue to love her with all of her imperfections, all of her needs and all of her baggage because I will teach you." Carmen will come home with lots of these things.

I sit here typing this with a grin because, yet again, this tiny imperfect soul has rocked my world and God grew a size bigger in my heart today because of her. She is indeed a life-giving giant disguised as a miniature, flawed package!

See, we all are lacking. We all have needs and baggage and imperfections. We all have problems and we all have marks. And God doesn't withhold His love until we finally get our act together and go next level. "But God demonstrates his own love for us in this: While we were still sinners, Christ died for us." (Romans 5:8)

I'm going to be overly transparent right now. I know that God loves me. I know that God loved me first. And I know that God cares for me despite my many flaws. But tonight it hit me a bit harder.

God told me He will teach me how to GIVE this kind of love. And as a follower of Jesus, this is something we all can do. I've seen it! And yet, I've been hiding.

I have not been to church in four months. I fear going to the grocery store because I might run across someone I know and perhaps I'll be unprepared or having an off day.

I might not have all the answers. What if I cry? What if I don't have the energy? What if I seem too sad or too happy? What if I am not perfect?

This was a hard realization for me because in this horribly imperfect circumstance, I once again forgot that I am more than the bad days and the unanswered questions. I am more than the what ifs and the ugly crying. I am more than a mother and more than a wife. I am more than the problems and imperfections in and around me.

God will teach me, and you, to love unconditionally because He loves us unconditionally. And, better yet, He wants us to love one another as He loves us!

So into the world I will go. Whether it's to the grocery store, church, the other side of the state, or the other side of the world, I will love and be loved.

"Beloved, if God so loved us, we also ought to love one another. No one has ever seen God; if we love one another, God abides in us and his love is perfected in us." (1 John 4:11-12)

March 13th, 2018

Carmen continues to have a tremendous amount of reflux.

While she remains fed through her intestines, she is still able to vomit gastric fluid. This is a big problem for many reasons. For starters, Carmen cannot grow if she cannot keep down what she is fed. Next, she does not protect her airway well and due to her paralyzed vocal cord she can easily compromise her lungs. And finally, this issue will keep her in the PICU until resolved.

This week we heard several opinions and options for Carmen with various timelines and surgeries.

Today the first step was taken by beginning a 24-hour test where a probe was inserted to help determine when and possibly why she is refluxing so much. So far she has hated the test and will be receiving another blood transfusion momentarily.

Over the next few days we will hear from surgeons at Children's National in Washington, DC regarding their recommendations. They will see if one of their surgeons feels comfortable operating on Carmen.

Her size is still a major obstacle. Operating on a tiny stomach that is even smaller from never actually having food in it magnifies the challenge.

She has fought so hard and I know she will continue to push through each battle Carmen-style!

March 14th, 2018

Mommy and Daddy got to visit Carmen tonight at the same time, which is extremely rare!

Carmen is still gagging a lot but we will have to wait until tomorrow to receive the results of yesterday's test.

We did some experimenting with Carmen's positions tonight. I know it may not seem like a lot but this was the first time I got to hold Carmen up on my shoulder!

Even being in the upright position was hard on her and it was pretty obvious she was dizzy. However, she held her own and did very well. I couldn't help but to wear a huge smile! Although Carmen was in discomfort it felt so nice to have her that close to me for a few minutes.

March 15th, 2018

Carmen is 15 weeks old today!

It's been 105 days and today is the 15th! Must be a blessed week!

By now you can probably see I have a thing for numbers and coordinating dates or any combination of the two. My lucky numbers are 2 and 3.

Almost everything happens to me in 2s and 3s — you'll just have to trust me on it.

I also apparently have a thing for writing. I never thought I was particularly good at it and honestly if it weren't for spell-check and autocorrect, I would have never written a single sentence in my life! I am truly the world's worst speller. My parents can testify.

Over the last few months I have been told, "You should start a blog! Write a book! What a great author you would be!" I'm not bragging. Because, once again, this was never something I thought I *would* do, *could* do, or even *wanted* to do. Believe me when I tell you, if I were to have laid out some sort of writing journey I would have chosen a completely different set of circumstances and resulting topic!

Tonight I was going through some paperwork and came across the information handed to me 13 weeks ago. It was the "road map" for Carmen's life. I remember reading those papers with such disdain. I hated what they said. I hated what they didn't say. And I hated that it was all confined to a few sheets of paper.

I decided to make the sign taped outside Carmen's door for a few reasons. One reason was that maybe some other parent would walk by and read, "Hi, my name is Carmen! I have been in the ICU for ___ days!" And think, "Finally! I've found someone in similar shoes! Maybe I can talk to her mother and see/tell her what's to come!" I also made it because even though the sign says how long she has been in the hospital, the numbers correspond with how long she has been alive and each day is a gift.

I know that Carmen's journey will be completely hers. Even if there *were* another person in the world with her same diagnosis, they would still be very different. But, how I would have loved to know I was not alone. I would have loved to be hopeful, to know I was not crazy, to know how to be an okay mom within hospital walls.

So, I have decided to write a book about our journey. It will be a mixture of medicine and miracles. I am not sure if that will be the title but it sounded fitting for now. It will have all of my journal entries from the beginning as well as pictures! It will also include all of Carmen's medical information.

My desire is that this book would be an encouragement to parents who have received a prenatal or postnatal diagnosis, and for those who have a multitude of medical complexities. My hope is that this book would be a resource available for parents doing life in the hospital alongside their child and the friends and family supporting them.

All the glory is His. Luck has nothing to do with it.

March 16th, 2018

I just got a call from one of the doctors in order to give me an update.

Carmen's central line will most likely come out today. They are becoming increasingly concerned that she will get another infection while they wait and are eager to remove it for right away.

Carmen is taking formula at a rate of 21 ml/hour! For her this is the first time that she has ever been at "full feeds," so she doesn't need other nutrients currently. Because they are feeding her intestines, what she is refluxing is not her feeds, but gastric fluid and secretions. Right now there is no direct correlation between what they feed her and what she spits up.

The doctor said that presently we are walking in "no man's land." Every doctor and surgeon agrees that Carmen will need to have stomach surgery with a G-tube placement, but no one feels comfortable enough to do it. So we wait.

Dr. C. has not given up and is still actively involved and pursuing a solution. Carmen's team does not feel they have exhausted all of their options in this area but will keep looking.

So I will remain hopeful that Carmen will be able to grow with her current ND feeding tube and someone will be able to help according to *her* perfect timing.

This might sound crazy, but I feel a little excited, though I can't quite put my finger on why. Maybe my sad and happy reactions are confused but I just can't wait to get this line out of her so I can hold her more easily and walk around with her — even if it is just in the hospital!

March 17th, 2018

This just happened!!!

After hours of preparation we left the room on day 107!
Though we had to come back fairly quickly it was exhilarating! Carmen did so well and even spread some lucky St. Patrick's Day cheer! I am so proud of this munchkin!!!

Nate, I wish you were here!

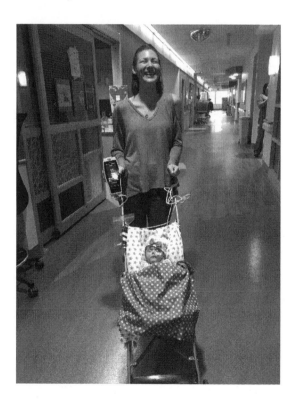

March 19th, 2018 (Morning)

I am blessed to have these moments.

It was a very difficult decision to leave Carmen and travel out of state to see my grandfather one last time. He had a cancerous brain tumor removed the same week as Carmen's first open-heart surgery and now God is calling him home.

In a way it was easy to leave Carmen because she has taught me that it isn't this life that matters. She taught me to spend time where you feel your heart leading.

Thank you, Jesus. Thank God for this man — my precious grandfather — who has always been a rock for our family. This is the man who took me to church and paid for my education. He was a man who changed the meaning of retiring and has been our example of honor and great leadership. We are proud to have your fingerprints on our lives! I know not everyone gets time to say goodbye to those they love. I will treasure these next days forever.

Thanks to all who have prayed for our family. The coming days will be very difficult, but we look forward to the end of suffering and one day being reunited in heaven one day. "Scatter kindness," he keeps saying. We will, Granddaddy. We will.

March 19th, 2018 (Afternoon)

My little prayer warrior!

Thank God for Mimi and Gigi who are home taking care of Holland's needs as well as Carmen in the hospital. Nate and I are so grateful to be able to see my granddaddy! Carmen's nurses made this so much easier by giving her extra love and attention today. They even sent me pictures!

Carmen gave her first smile without tons of meds today! I am sad I missed it but I got to show my granddad a photo and it looks like she is praying for us, too! What a gift!

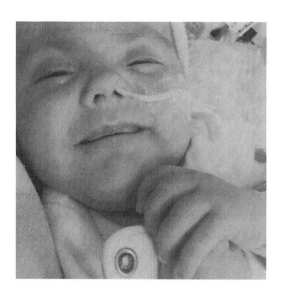

March 21st, 2018

I am so proud of this little champion!

After 16 weeks, Carmen is scheduled to leave the PICU tomorrow and go to the step-down unit!

She was supposed to leave today but there were some staffing issues causing a delay. Carmen needs to be paired with nurses whose patients aren't in isolation.

This is a huge step for all of us. Carmen has only known life inside the PICU.

Mommy is spending the night with little peanut before she "graduates" tomorrow. While the next steps for Carmen are still unclear, we will count this as the victory it is! Prayers are for a smooth transition. Carmen got a real bath tonight without all her "tentacles." Mommy got to hold her as a free woman!

March 22nd, 2018

Today I awoke in the hospital after a few hours of broken sleep to the sound of morning rounds.

I didn't want to miss this, so I jumped up from my chair and opened the door to 15 members of Carmen's team. Despite my grogginess I was excited since it's moving day for Carmen!

It was a strange feeling because I felt like we were missing something. And apparently I wasn't the only one.

After I heard the doctors voice prospective plans that had no set direction the debates began, yet again, about what Carmen specifically needs and what she can and can't do. I locked eyes with one of her cardiologists and asked if we could please try and feed her stomach. Until we know for sure what she is capable of, we will never know what is actually the best course of action to take.

I expressed that I needed to see for myself that she couldn't do something before she goes through yet another surgery. We have to give her a chance.

I was surprised and delighted with just how amazing many of the doctors were. Despite being a bit skeptical they were hopeful and prepared to discover the answer in the face of what appears to be limited options.

At 9:15 AM Carmen began receiving trickles of formula in her stomach for the first time in four months.

We are now up to 5 ml/hour without one single gag thus far. I don't know how far she will be able to go, but I know without a doubt that we had to leave it up to her. We had to be bold!
For the last six hours I have held her and stared at her, jumping at every tiny noise to see if she is okay.

Today I feel like Carmen's mother. I feel like I am doing my part to help and protect her but also to challenge and support her.

I am so proud of you, baby girl!

March 23rd, 2018

Carmen is doing exceedingly well!

She has been a bit cranky but we think her tummy might be hurting as it gets used to this new way of feeding. She is up to 14 ml/hour!!!

I am so very happy!!! Slow and steady, baby girl! Carmen got to see Mimi tonight and has a new nickname: Pebbles! (Because of her silly ponytail!)

March 24th, 2018

Carmen started throwing up again last night.

She was able to tolerate 16 ml/hour, but nothing more. She is being taken downstairs for another GI test right now.

I haven't slept in 30 hours. Holland was up all night and developed a really bad rash to the point where her skin is peeling. I took Holland to the doctor this morning and she is now on antibiotics, numbing cream, and medicated ointment. They don't know precisely what the cause is but they are treating it like a chemical burn. Poor baby!

When we were in the doctor's office, Holland assumed we were at the hospital and began looking for Carmen. It was pretty pathetic and we both started crying. Some days I feel like the worst mom in the world. I need about seven more hands.

March 25th, 2018

Today has been a busy day at the hospital. I don't know if this is good or bad news, but it's just where we are at this very moment.

Carmen did not tolerate full feeds in her stomach and her lungs are "wet" again. She is being fed once again in her intestines and although a lot of good came out of her trying to feed in her stomach, it is just not an option for her at this juncture.

So, next steps...

The general consensus at INOVA, Children's National, and specialists from Walter Reed agree that it is in Carmen's best interest to wait and grow to 5 kg, a little over 11 pounds, before she can receive a *Nissen Fundoplication*. This is a surgical procedure in which the top of the stomach is wrapped around itself to prevent reflux.

Carmen is currently 3.5 kg and if she doesn't have any setbacks, it's possible she could be a candidate for surgery in a month.

As much as I want her home, I feel that Carmen should stay at INOVA for treatment. Transferring her would pose many risks and we are unsure if she would receive treatment any sooner at another facility. We have decided to make the best of the wait and believe that time alone could have many positive benefits for her.

143

I have asked to have all of Carmen's primary team members agree together that this is in fact the best decision. My hope is that we can come up with a schedule for Carmen and create a list of goals and milestones to achieve while we wait. I will push for written consent that when Carmen reaches 5 kg, she will be considered for a Nissen Fundoplication and G-tube surgery without delay.

March 25th, 2018

I was feeling a bit hopeless today.

I decided to make a board of Carmen's progress from birth to now. I didn't know making posters could be a form of therapy but here we are. I am so excited to bring this to the PICU tomorrow!

I have really tried to celebrate all that I could within these walls and I hope this poster will be helpful to her providers. I hope it is a reminder that Carmen is an individual who has overcome much!

March 26th, 2018

After 117 days, Carmen is now on what we are calling a "stay-cation" out of the PICU!

She is now in IMC (Intermediate Care) in a big, bright, beautiful room!

Because Carmen cannot go home yet, we have all decided that this step-down unit will be better for her to be able to wait and grow for her next surgery.

The reason Carmen can't go home is because she is fed ND. This means the feeding tube that goes through her nose passes through her stomach into her intestines. This needs to be in the correct position so that she does not aspirate. Carmen is fairly skilled at removing this tube and if we were home and it came out, it could be very dangerous for her and would necessitate a trip to the ER.

In the IMC she will have a more relaxing environment with less strict rules. She can have more visitors and will be able to do more baby things.

While this isn't exactly where we would like to be, we are excited for what this small step will be like for Carmen.

Also, for the first time since birth, Carmen is being fed Mama's milk! Time to chunk up, little one!

March 27th, 2018

We have learned to seize every opportunity to spend quality time together. Now that Carmen is on the step-down unit, she is able to have more visitors. Holland is able to come see her sister here whenever she can!

I think Holland could be a great doctor one day. And, yes, they are in matching outfits!

March 28th, 2018 (Morning)

Carmen, meet natural light…

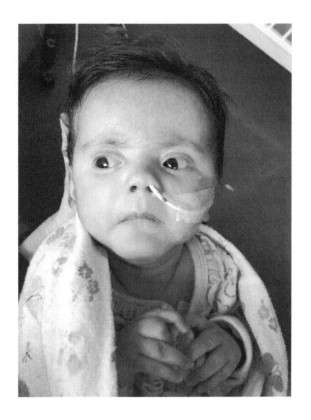

March 28th, 2018 (Evening)

Tonight I hold you with many emotions.

Some moments I can't believe we are still in the hospital, and others I can't believe how far you've come.

As I sit here and hold you in the dark, I have the door wide open. Both you and I aren't used to the quietness outside of the PICU. There is a little boy being discharged from his 10-day stay in the hospital.

His grandpa whispers to his grandson, "Wave bye to Carmen, **the PICU baby**." The boy says, "Bye, Carmen!"
And the grandpa says, "I know we will hear of her again some day."

I don't know what he meant but I know that I am happy for them and they are happy for Carmen. I know that they are aware of how long she has been here, and I know they can't believe how far she's come. More than that, I am sure they will hear of her again. I am sure of it!

I've never felt stronger than when I'm holding you, my love.

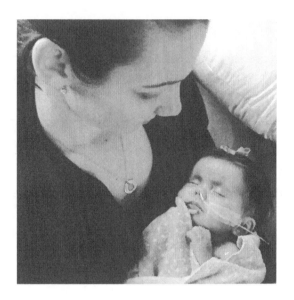

March 29th, 2018

Granddaddy went to be with the Lord early this morning.

While his presence in this world is deeply missed, his legacy is felt even now.

What an incredible man of God! Humble, kind, selfless, smart, and intentional. We are blessed and comforted knowing that you are experiencing ultimate joy.

In his honor we will be spreading acts of kindness today! I have packed a bunch of gift baskets to bring to the nurses at the hospital. So many people have blessed us with goodies over these months and I know firsthand how a beautiful gift basket has made me feel!

I love you, Granddaddy!

Thank you for everything you have instilled in my family and me. I am confident in how one gets to heaven, so I know that is where you are. Your faith astounds me.

March 31st, 2018 (Afternoon)

Carmen decided to pull her ND tube almost all the way off of her face today.

So.... I did what any normal parent would do.

I pulled the rest of the tube out, washed her face, got her dressed and did a photo-shoot without the stupid tube. It's not stupid, but you get it.

Of course, I then informed her nurse that it needed to be replaced.

March 31st, 2018 (Evening)

Seasons...

I have to admit, as much as I love spring, I have been tempted to hold my breath in protest over its arrival this year.

My fall baby who spent two seasons in the hospital will now enter a new season. A season yet again I didn't know would be within these walls.

Sometimes I feel like my world stopped in autumn. It's almost a sickening feeling to see flowers bloom and not need a winter coat.

I tried to hold on to autumn. I tried to keep it and maybe wake up again when it was still autumn and she would be home. We could have the holidays together like we were "supposed to." We could watch Holland open her Christmas gifts as Carmen slept in my arms by the fire. We could count down to the New Year in the same room and wake up all night long to nurse the new baby. We could spend birthdays together and do everything under the sky that families do in winter.

Life goes on in both its beauty and torment.

When I scroll through my phone and see a picture of my face before we knew what was ahead, I cringe.

I don't know why, but I always think to myself, "How stupid was she? How ungrateful was she? How did she dare to smile? Oh, she didn't know."

She didn't know how to hurt, and she didn't know how to lose. She didn't know how to see the pain and dissect it. She didn't know tired and hungry and ugly.

She didn't know what she could do. She didn't know how to love. She didn't know how to help. She just didn't know.

There are days where I transfer that view of myself to others. I hate it, but I have heard that it's natural. I see moms complain just like I did. I see tiny babies journey home to sleep in love-filled rooms with Mommy and Daddy like we did with Holland. I see bliss and energy and I see people who don't know what they are truly capable of.

To know I will never be able to go back and be that girl is unsettling. Every decision and every day is changed forever.

Forever is unlike a season, it remains. Its stillness covers the snow and the flowers and blends them together until there is no discernible separation.

Some people don't believe in forever, but I do. In fact, these months have taught me to not only believe in forever, but to seek and anticipate it. Prepare for and crave it!

And seasons... they will come and go.

There is a time for planting and a time for blooming, a time for stillness and a time for music, a time for darkness and a time for light.

Today I am thankful for forever and for where my forever lies. And today I think... I am thankful for seasons.

For just like the plants, little one, your fall and winter were dark and stagnant. There was loss and rest, but spring my dear, has come.

April

FOOLS

April 1st, 2018

Happy Easter from the Hatchers!

Carmen absolutely hated this outfit, but I just had to dress her up in it. This is also the very same outfit Holland wore for her first Easter!

April 2nd, 2018

Today was such a great day!

It has been fascinating to watch Carmen finally getting the opportunity to be a baby! Exhaustion, surgery, sedation and recovery took up all of Carmen's time and energy for the beginning months of her life. Now it is as if she is a brand new baby.

Her adjusted age varies and lies somewhere between two weeks and two months even though she is over four months old. We have been working with multiple therapists to help Carmen build muscle and strength as well as assist her in relearning things that are no longer reflexive, such as swallowing.

We worked this week on a schedule for Carmen to best enable her to rest and grow. Living in the hospital has been a challenge but we are so thankful for Carmen's team as they wholeheartedly try to make the best of everything!

Carmen is adjusting to natural light, has been gaining weight, and even enjoyed a bath this evening!

Over the next week, Carmen's vision and hearing will be analyzed since proper testing couldn't be done initially. Also, custom splints will be formed for Carmen's thumbs, which seem to have a slightly different anatomy.

While Carmen fell asleep, Mommy and Mimi rearranged her hospital room. I hope the nurses don't mind the changes but it's much more homey now.

This little girl is truly a gift to Mommy and Daddy. She really did come to the perfect family. We are so excited to learn and grow with her every step of the way!

April 5th, 2018

Happy 19 weeks, sweet pea!

This week her weight is staying right around 8 pounds. We still have quite a way to **GrOw** (see what I did there?) but progress is certainly being made. One thing (or group of things) that has continued growing is that beautiful hair of hers!

Carmen will still be in the hospital for the foreseeable future as we await her next surgery. In the meantime, Carmen is being weaned off the many medications she has been on and it seems that each day a new version of this angelic treasure emerges!

Some days Carmen is completely out of it and exhausted, and others she is restless and irritated. She spends her time trying to rest and grow. Carmen has been able to go on a few stroller rides around the 8th floor, snuggle with family and friends, sit in her bouncer, lay on a play mat, have all sorts of therapy, and even make art!
We are so proud of you, Carmen!

April 9th, 2018

After therapy Carmen fell asleep holding her cat.

Her therapist was very happy considering how rigorous these last few days have been. She is beginning to semi-purposely open and close her hands on things. I praise the Lord for these little victories.

April 11th, 2018

Shout-out to Little Miss Holland!

At just over two years old, Holland is truly wonderful. She has had a difficult several months adjusting to our family of four and has spent lots of days away from Mommy and Daddy, or in and out of the hospital.

Through everything she stays remarkably strong. She makes me laugh on days I never thought I could smile and she has taught me to keep going no matter what. She is bright, kind, empathetic and sometimes hilarious. Every step of the way she is right by our side. Holland hugs me when I am in tears and wants to do everything we do to help Carmen.

Last night was no different. Nate and I were practicing infant CPR and Holland surprised us by jumping right in!
I know God picked you to be the best big sister for baby Carmen.

April 12th, 2018

She's really doing it!!!

Wow! Twenty weeks. Five months in the hospital.
We have had quite the journey and our destination still has no ETA, but that's okay!

Carmen is actually doing very well. She was hanging at the 8-pound mark for a while but after increasing her feed volume and managing her withdrawal symptoms, she is now 8 pounds, 4 ounces! I am so proud of her!

This last week we received some disturbing news about a test result. This is the third time Carmen's blood work has tested positive for SCID, which stands for *Severe Combined Immunodeficiency*. If accurate, it could alter every part of how Carmen lives her life.

Instead of surrendering to the waves of bad news by lying in a heap and crying, I have chosen to celebrate all of the good things I can see and somehow take hold of them.

Last night, Carmen was very alert and calm, a mixture that is rare for her. She began to lift her arms, somewhat purposely, and touch my face. I thought it had to be a mistake but the nurse saw her do it as well and said she believes she is trying to reach out for me.

This may not seem like a big deal, but for months Carmen would not even move her arms away from her body since she instinctively protects her sternum. A lot of babies take a long time to release that need for protection so I am glad she is feeling more comfortable.

Carmen moved to a new room yesterday and will continue to do so every two weeks for infection prevention.

April 14th, 2018 (Morning)

After a few days of contemplation, we believe Carmen is actually trying to smile and make noises!

She is doing fabulously and, my goodness, I think the day she gives me a non-drugged-out grin will be one of the best days of my life! She really has turned a corner!

April 14th, 2018 (Afternoon)

After 142 days, Carmen got to go outside!!

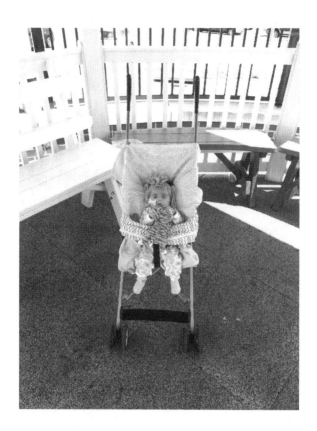

April 19th, 2018

Happy 21 weeks, Carmen!

Not many new developments to share at the moment but our primary concerns, and what we are praying for, are as follows:

- That she continues to gain weight and tolerate her feeds. She is now up to 23 ml/hour!
- That the rigors associated with the medication weaning process would ease up for her.
- That her team would have fruitful conversations with possible surgeons for Carmen's Nissen Fundoplication and G-tube surgery.
- That the pending test results on her immune system function would be favorable.
- That our family is able to shift gears should Carmen be transferred to another hospital if that is what is deemed best for her care.

April 20th, 2018

Last night I began to feel anxious.

In three weeks Carmen will have been in the hospital for six months. Half a year!

And to think it will be more than half a year is just… I really don't know. How did we even get here? Sometimes the days feel so terribly long.

I looked back at the first few days when we thought Carmen would be home by Christmas. I think if someone would have told me, "Ma'am, in half a year, you will still be here," I would have fallen on my face and never gotten up again.

But today is all we have. Maybe even just for the moment. Today is all we are told to concern ourselves with (Matthew 6:34). Tomorrow will come. And the strength and knowledge will come for that day when we need it.

To go back and look at pictures makes me so proud of how far Carmen has come.

Holding her then, part of me wishes I knew that in six months she would still be alive; that we would still be okay, still have tomorrow, and that she'd still fit perfectly in my hands.

No day is guaranteed.

April 22nd, 2018

Day 150.

I love my husband. I don't tell him enough. It's hard to speak to each other most days. We are on the same team but it often feels like he plays at home and I play on the travel team. We bark words in passing and hope the other one will read between the lines.

He is a very good father and I know he would be here more if he could.

Watching them sleep together gave me great peace. Sometimes words are pointless, anyway.

April 23rd, 2018

Today I cried a lot.

First of all, I hadn't had much sleep, once again had a crick in my neck, and my jaw was aching from clenching my teeth throughout the night. I was angry that I started the day this way.

Secondly, I cried because I opted for my "uniform" of black and gray despite all the beautiful clothes I have in my closet. I put back a large sweater only because I could hear my mother's voice in my head saying, "Sydney! It's April, for crying out loud!" I was angry because I removed my earrings because I felt they were just too much for my life right now. I don't want to stand out. I don't want to be uncomfortable. I don't want to look pretty. I don't feel pretty.

Today I decided to actually look at myself in the mirror. I mean *all* of myself. I was wearing leggings and in my mind I looked different. Radically different, actually. *Better* different. I didn't realize my baby pouch was that noticeable. I didn't think my breasts were that, say, non-existent. I don't think I can even begin to describe my shape.

My eyes looked very tired. My skin is awful again and my postpartum hair loss is pretty apparent on the left side. I have a lot of gray hair, too. My teeth feel very crowded and I should go to the dentist soon. After this lovely review, I was actually glad I was wearing leggings!

I was surprised how much of my current body was new news to me, yet I was less than shocked that it was my reality. Some days I wonder how I still shower, brush my teeth, and get dressed. Want to know a little secret? Some days I don't. Of course, that's just between you and me.

Anyway. I went to a social gathering this afternoon and three times during the event I thought to myself, "I can't do this!" There has been very few times over the last six months that I have done something not involving the hospital. I barely know how to carry a conversation that doesn't include life-saving terminology.

My heart was beating very fast and I found myself either unable to keep up with the conversation or intermittently stopped listening so that I could make up other scenarios in my head. Ten seconds later I could rejoin the discussion like nothing happened.

I ended up in a conversation about anxiety and I was thrown back to the memory of the long night in February when I collapsed at the hospital due to stress. I was completely unconscious and drooling and my whole body convulsed for hours after. I am so ashamed of this memory and I do my best to not let it have power over me. I moved on to other conversations and ended up being very grateful to have gone.

As I drove to the hospital, a migraine came on. I toyed with the idea of stopping to buy some pain meds, but was too anxious and needed to get to Carmen.

I arrived and was disappointed yet again with a bunch of things. This week has been very frustrating at the hospital and I just wanted to push through.

I put some hot towels on my neck and chugged some iced coffee, ready to be nurse/mommy to my baby girl.

I stayed for a "brief" stay of four and a half hours and once Carmen was happily asleep I made my 45-minute journey back home.

As I got on the interstate my gaslight came on. I tensed up because I felt like it was mocking me. I shushed the voice in my head that was pleading, "Sydney, you need to take a break, you don't have to do this." And so I kept driving.

When I got to the gas station I was sure to avoid eye contact with anyone. Wouldn't it be the absolute worst if someone smiled at me this very moment? What kind of expression would I return? Remember what your face looks like, Sydney! Goodness, that would be awful.

I turned on the radio and started to think that maybe I smile too much, actually. And so I started to cry.

I don't even know why. I felt alone, abandoned, frustrated, and, oddly enough, like I was too nice. I thought about a comment that was made to me earlier that day: "You must hate everyone who has a perfect life."

I love the person who made the comment and I recall several other people who have stated the same phrase to me recently. I didn't really know how to respond but I started thinking about how I should take this. I don't want anyone to think I hate him or her. No one has a perfect life. Even Jesus, who was the perfect human being, had nothing remotely resembling what most around us consider the ideal life. And He made a point out of seeking out and hanging with flawed, marginalized, and victimized people. My brain went on this tangent for some time until I was home.

I cooked, ate, cleaned up, watched a strange movie, and then called the hospital for my nightly check. More frustrating news was given and I felt the bubble form in my chest.

Once everyone was in their beds, I sat on the couch and tried to cry as silently as I could. I thought I was probably doing myself a disservice because crying in that way is kind of painful and most likely doesn't release anything. I began messaging a friend to vent and slowly descended from my silent emotional breakdown.

I tried to reason over my frustrations and come up with a "mama bear" plan of action for the next week. I thought about how badly I want to help others. Yet, I am still in this place of needing. It reminded me what a blessing it is to be able to help and to give.

I know I will have days, months and perhaps even entire years like that again, but right now my internal gas light is flashing. No matter how fast I want to get from point A to point B, I have to stop and fill up before I start the journey

That's actually a good illustration of how I feel — like a dilapidated car that is constantly running on fumes. I feel dirty and outdated, most likely needing lots of work and lacking the features that can make travelling by auto easy and comfortable.

I feel like I know where I want to go and some days I have precise directions to get there. But I am stuck.

I feel like I am a good enough car, one that has gone through a few fender benders, but has really proven to be good and dependable. It's just that I'm trying run on empty; nothing left in the tank.

As I write this, I kind of see my problem and a possible solution.

We are mind, body and soul.
I feel like I talk to Jesus every second. I feel like I am filling my mind and soul with His word. I feel like I am exercising my mind in ways to protect it from most evil thoughts and even make it stronger by learning as much as I can during this season.

But my body is weak; it has been pushed away and uncared for. It has been sacrificed — bumped to last place — and could quite possibly be affecting the whole trifecta!

April 25th, 2018

We have entered a different battlefront in Carmen's life.

As much as I would love to share all of the details, I feel it is wise to wait until I have more concrete information.

We have requested prayers for great wisdom for Nate, me, and our family. Prayers for the facilitation of valuable meetings and the best use of time. Prayers for Carmen's still pending immune system results, her blood clots, and new heart findings. Prayers that she will continue to gain weight and build strength.

We have even requested that those bold enough might pray for Carmen's esophagus and stomach, for her reflux to be healed, and for her stomach to miraculously grow!

Carmen is 9 pounds as of today! She had her second attempted hearing test but it was deemed unsuccessful.

I think I am starting to find my real voice.

April 25th, 2018

Most are familiar with the saying," When one door closes, another will open."

Well, what if there really is only one door? Some days I feel like I'm in a very stark room with four walls and a single door labeled "no more options." I look at that door and know what it means and resent that it's the only one. Some days I just stare at that door, anxious about the day I will open it.

But this week I learned that there are multiple ways to play this game. I was too busy staring at the "no options" door that I forgot to look in my bag and reach for the ax I've had all along.

Sure, I have an ax. Everyone has an ax. We don't want to use it. We forget we have it. We pretend not to have it. Well, I found my ax anyway and suddenly there wasn't just one way to go. The walls (even the ceiling) couldn't hold me anymore! And even though I have to be careful with this ax, it's a real game-changer.

To be honest I don't know how to use this thing, but I am a bit excited for the possibilities it affords me.

See, not everyone knows how to be strong and fight a battle they never wanted to fight with a strength they never knew they had. Until, that is, it's the only option.

April 26th, 2018

It has been very difficult to try and share everything over the last few days but I just wanted to thank everyone who has prayed for Carmen.

This is a very critical time for her as we are in an awkward waiting period. Nothing new that Carmen will need to have a Nissen Fundiplication surgery with a G-tube placement. The risks of her going through this procedure, however, are still too great at this time. We are working very closely with numerous specialists to assess the risks and benefits and are attempting to draw up a prospective timeline with Carmen's safety and well being in mind. There is no perfect solution.

As her parent, it has been very difficult to learn so much in such a short amount of time and try to decide what is best for her. Each day I feel a little bit more overwhelmed yet capable. Each day I feel myself stepping up to the challenge at hand, even if those days are filled with tears, frustration, and confusion. I feel more ready than ever to be the best medical-mother to Carmen.

I know, as always, Carmen will show us one way or the other what she truly needs. We are trying to be very wise and take hundreds of things into consideration when talking about next steps. But there are a few lingering things that Carmen will need to smooth out before any decisions are made.

Carmen has been more awake and aware as of late. Everyday I feel like I am meeting her for the first time.

We are still waiting for Carmen's immune system results that will greatly impact whether or not she goes to surgery.

Carmen has been refluxing frequently which can always put her lungs in danger and she is also getting her first teeth! Yay? This is both exciting and nerve-racking. Carmen does not know how to swallow well and she is gagging and spitting up more due to teething-induced excess saliva. The ND tube going into her throat doesn't help the situation, either.

Carmen is now taking in formula at a rate of 27 ml/hour. The breast milk stash that I was able to produce in the first six weeks of her life is all used up and hospital policies do not allow Carmen to receive donor milk.

This week Carmen had a repeat sonogram, lasting almost three hours, to determine the status of her blood clots, but no new information emerged. She also had a repeat echocardiogram because the pulses in her lower extremities have been less than in her upper regions. The echo revealed a narrowing in one of the valves in the lower part of her heart but it is not posing any risks to her at present, and may never become a threat. If that occurs this could be something managed in the catheterization lab.

The most recent changes to Carmen's health have resulted in faster breathing and a few episodes of desaturations. This means oxygen-rich blood is not flowing out of her heart as well to the rest of her body. She has not had either of these issues in 45 days, so we are eager to get her back on track.

I know this was a ton of information, so it is all I will share for now.

April 27th, 2018

What a horrible night.

I haven't left the hospital in 20 hours. Carmen is back on high-flow oxygen support after six weeks of perfect circulation. She was in the 40s and 50s multiple times last night and no one knows why. This feels like a punch in the gut and four steps back.

The night was filled with confusion, frustration, and anger. I am so exhausted but need to keep fighting. It breaks my heart to see Carmen like this after knowing what she is capable of.

There were so many issues and mistakes over the last two days that have left us discouraged. I am pleading for Carmen's strength today and for her team and me as we attempt to uncover the reasons behind her sudden decline.

April 28th, 2018 (Afternoon)

Nate and I have been at the hospital around the clock for the last three days and are exhausted.

Thank God for our mothers who have taken care of Holland while we are here.

It would be unfair for me to write a medical update at this time because there are still many unknowns and we are doing our best to help Carmen as we try not to be overwhelmed by anxiety.

Carmen is a mighty warrior and we believe she has been under some unnecessary stress for a while and numerous things have resulted in her current state. We know we cannot change the past but we are striving to change her future!

Not having answers have made the last two days rough. While Carmen is on some extra support right now, we are trying to stay positive and allow her body to rest and recover. Her team has made various changes and everyone is doing their part in making sure her needs are being met more appropriately.

Today a few new faces have seen Carmen and throughout the day we will be meeting with other specialists to gain a better understanding of what her next steps should be.

Carmen is still in the step-down unit and has not been transferred back to the PICU. Her care is being managed and she has both teams working alongside one another. If any other interventions are needed, Carmen will have to be moved back to the PICU.

After a fairly decent day and night of rest, Carmen is awake and alert at the moment. It is always a blessing to see her keep going. There have been moments where we feel so discouraged and then, all of a sudden, she will somehow show us she is not giving up.

We aren't giving up either, baby girl!

April 28th, 2018 (Night)

This is what self-care looks like. This is called, "I finally left the hospital because if I didn't I would most likely become a patient myself." Again.

I have been wearing Nate's pants for who knows how long and my legs ache. I went to the drive-thru at McDonalds and I think that was probably the best decision I've made all day.

This is what surrender looks like for me. This isn't giving up; this is me trying to be a good mom. This isn't the best version of myself; I mean, seriously, I wish this wasn't a version of myself at all. I don't even know who I am anymore. I am empty and I can't do this. No one can do this.

We are encouraged to go on a date, to take time for ourselves, to do something that makes us happy. Though I know this is offered with the very best of intentions, I consider this to be the most unrealistic advice anyone can offer right now. Each day my life is like a fire drill. I bring with me what is necessary and I don't care what I look like. I am constantly on edge and constantly trying to find what is important.

Nate walked in to see me feet- up on the couch, stuffing a cheeseburger in my mouth and he was proud of me. I know it doesn't seem like much, but this is my self care.

April 29th, 2018 (After midnight)

As of 1 AM Carmen has been transferred back to the PICU.

She has tachycardia and is undergoing numerous tests. I have no answer at this time but I have a peace knowing she is back in the unit that knows her very well.

April 29th, 2018 (Morning)

As I made my way into the hospital today, two of the songs that have helped me get through these very dark days came on the radio.

Just about every day this winter, Lauren Daigle's "Trust in You" and Hillary Scott's "Thy Will" played. They became my anthems for Carmen.

I tried my best not to cry. I didn't know how it would feel to walk back into the same room where she recovered from her major surgeries. I didn't know what she would look like or what she would do. I turned the radio all the way up and was screaming along to the songs, reminding myself that we just have to keep going.

Back in her previous room she seemed bigger. I hated seeing the many lines in her again and knowing she was on extra support that she hasn't needed in so long. It was also hard having no answers and coming to grips with the possibility that I would never know.

My mom was asleep in the chair next to her. They both looked so peaceful.

About an hour after I arrived, and while her tired body was receiving yet another blood transfusion, she awoke and smiled! She was smiling and moving all around more than ever before. She even had a little giggle! My mom and I were shocked! How can she go from *that* to *this*?

My heart is so full! Carmen, you are a miracle! I know you feel our prayers! Keep going, little one. Mommy is right here!

May

HALF A YEAR, MUCH TO CELEBRATE

May 1st, 2018

It has been a tough journey and I honestly never thought I would share as much as I have in such an open and publically accessible manner.

Some days I feel there is no way I can continue to write, that it's just too much and I should give it up. I do not want people to feel sorry for us. Carmen is one of the most profound blessings I have ever received and our entire family is stronger because of her. Her story is having a massive impact and the thought of even just one person being helped inspires me to keep writing. So I soldier on!

We had an important meeting yesterday with 15 of Carmen's providers. Like always, everything is challenging. There are many steps and many questions that still need to be answered. As much as we didn't want to hear this news, it is now on the table that Carmen's heart will need further investigation.

It is difficult to know right now if the aspirations caused her lungs to become sick and is in turn making her heart function worse, or if her heart would have needed additional repair as she grows, or even some combination of the two.

There were many other discussions, but this is where we will have to start. Unless something drastically changes soon, Carmen will go back to the catheterization lab on Thursday.

They will measure all of the pressures and flow in and out of her heart and, depending on what they find, some aspect of intervention could be done at that time. This means Carmen will be required to once again have central line access, be intubated, and go under general anesthesia. All of this is very risky because of the restricted access she has due to her blood clots and dysfunctional airway.

Either way, her aspirations are serious and with the severity of them, it could be more of a risk for her to NOT have the Nissen Fundoplication and G-tube surgery than it would be to wait. Her reflux is just too severe.

Plastic surgeons came to see Carmen today and explained that they would not perform jaw surgery on her because they do not believe that would help her in any way, which aligns with the earlier diagnosis. Because Carmen cannot handle the increased secretions brought on by teething, there is also the possibility that she could need a tracheotomy in the event it becomes an even more prominent issue. A trach has been on the table in the past and I have to accept that if it is what will be best for her, it can't be as horrible as I imagine.

These things will all be addressed in the order of what is most pressing, beginning with her heart.

I am dreading Thursday. I know that as Carmen gets older and more interactive, it will be more difficult to see her in a sedated state.

We will press on.

I was surprised at how I made it through the consultation without breaking down and as the meeting drew to a close I thanked everyone for being there and for not giving up on Carmen. Her main surgeon said, "It's not important that we aren't giving up on her.

The important thing is Carmen isn't giving up."

May 2nd, 2018

And so it begins…

Carmen has spent the day being prepped and kept as happy and resting as possible as she readies for tomorrow. She will be in the catheterization lab at 8 AM for her cardiologist to gather more information on the status of her heart. Depending on the findings, some aspects of intervention could be done at that time.

We are all very anxious because we expect that they will indeed find something and even pray that a reason *is* found. And yet we hope it is something that can be easily remedied. I am not one to take "I don't know" as an answer, but with Carmen a certain measure of uncertainty is always on the table.

For the last two days, I have had the biggest knot in my stomach. I have been pondering why God has brought us back to this place and even back to this very same room, as if it really is back to the beginning.

The word *endure* has become very apparent to me.

God, I have not forgotten the words you gave me.
We will NOT give up and we know that You WILL always be faithful. You have always been faithful!

We will persevere for whatever time you allow. We will continue to seek you and intend for You to receive ALL the glory! We are so blessed!

193

May 3rd, 2018

I cannot put all of today's findings into words yet but, as usual, today's seven-hour heart procedure was difficult and multi-faceted.

The intubation took a very long time. A team of six was needed to place her breathing tube. The cardiologist said it was the most difficult intubation he had ever seen. Getting access for lines was also very hard. These two steps alone took three hours.

A 20% gradient obstruction, from where Carmen's first heart surgery had healed, was removed via balloon dilation. The rest of the exploratory procedure is best explained at another time. I was told that it is fairly common that babies with the type of surgery Carmen originally had can end up having narrowing in the same spot and needing this intervention.

Around 3:30 PM I was able to see Carmen.

I hated seeing her that way again, but to me she seemed bigger. I could tell how strong she has become since I had seen her that way before.

She does have some trauma from the intubation and her heart rate was is high. She has a low-grade fever, but she did earlier as well. Carmen is currently receiving a blood transfusion. She is requiring a high amount of pain and sedation medication because she is so used to the dosages and is currently very aware and attempting to wriggle away and out from under her tubes.

They hope to keep her comfortable throughout the night, and be able to keep her intubated while they replace her ND feeding tube using interventional radiology tomorrow morning. The goal is to remove her breathing tube following the ND tube placement. They are trying to coordinate her teams before the weekend so that she will not have to wait in this state for long. Tonight will be difficult.

May 5th, 2018

The last two days as Carmen has been recovering from her heart procedure she has been very irritable and unwell.

While some of this was expected, we were just notified that Carmen actually has rhinovirus. This explains why her oxygen saturation is still on the lower end, why she is coughing and spitting up more, and running a fever. There is nothing to be done but let the virus run its course.

Carmen will continue to be in isolation and we hope she will be better by the end of the week. Because of her compromised immune system, we pray that Carmen can regain strength and successfully make the virus tap out before it develops into a serious threat.

Holland has also been a little under the weather so I have not been able to see Carmen the last two days in order to limit the passing of germs.

Mothering is hard sometimes! My girls have taught me to look for the good in every day and after what seems like a billion years, today I decided to cook. And it wasn't half bad!

Sometimes God creates situations where all you can do is tackle what is directly in front of you.

May 6th, 2018

Carmen is in isolation but Mommy got permission to see her this morning after two days!

We read poetry and had the worship music cranked up! Happy Sunday, everyone!

You absolutely cannot break a woman who seeks her happiness from God!

May 7th, 2018

Carmen is a bit of an overachiever. In less than a week she:

- Had a major heart procedure.
- Contracted a virus.
- Drove four teeth through. (Yes, four at once!)

And she is battling through it all like a champ!!!

And what did I do? Worry, complain, attempt to clean? Yes.

I love you Carmen! You are amazing! Thank you for always setting the bar high!

May 12th, 2018

Happy Mother's Day!

This year I have needed my mother more than the last ten years combined.

When Carmen decided to make her grand entrance early, my mom was there. When Nate had to work due to having just started a new job my mom was often there in the hospital with me. Bracing myself for terrifying news over and over, my mom was like an anchor keeping me from drifting into the abyss of despair. When the calls came telling me to get to the hospital right away, my mom was there for Holland and me.

When I had no energy left to cook, clean, or even tend to myself, she was there. She had an up close and personal view of everything each and very step of the way.

And I saw her.

I saw a love in her I had never seen before. I saw perseverance in her I had yet to notice. I saw a care in her greater than I had ever known.

Sometimes that was the hardest part. To see her sad and worried and hopeless was excruciating. But as moms, we did what moms do best. We took deep breaths, pulled out that brave face from deep down, and kept going. We did it for our daughters, we did it for our families, and we did it for ourselves.

Being a mom is the hardest role I've ever played. But this year I have had the strength of a million mothers because it's as if a million mothers have carried me through.

The days where I was hungry, the days I was angry, the days I was sure it was the last day I had; you moms saved me. My mom, stepmom, mother-in-law, grandmothers, aunts, sisters, cousins, friends, doctors, nurses, church members, and strangers saved me. Yes, YOU! Thank YOU!

There is no deeper earthy love that can be felt than the love of a mother. It is a bond that will go to great lengths and great depths, through fire and fear. It is a love that creates a smile when all anyone else can see are tears. It's a love that creates a meal for others when eating is the very last thing on your mind. It's a love that organizes everyone else's life, even when theirs is in tatters. It's a love the cheers when the crowd jeers. It's a love that gives love when she feels all of the love has already been given. It's a love that is never ending and ever growing.

This Mother's Day I don't want flowers or candy or even for someone to make me breakfast or clean the house. I don't want cards, poems, or gifts.

This Mother's Day I just want to thank each of you for being the most incredible mothers in the entire world. You have hearts of gold and are doing astounding things every day! You are fulfilling the greatest calling you will ever have! You are amazing and you are loved.

May 13th, 2018

This morning my mom made us all breakfast and we were given the green light to see Carmen for a bit. It has been five days since we have seen her because we were sick. As hard as we tried to kill all of the germs, all of us came down with the stomach flu.

We are all glad we stayed away from Carmen as she is still recovering and is doing much better! Happy Mommy's Day from Carmen!

May 14th, 2018

Happy Monday!

I am so excited to announce that Carmen is feeling better!

She is on room air with flow for just a bit of support. Her temperature has been in the normal range for three days and she even shared some of her spunky self today! I hope everyone else can find his or her spunk today!

May 17th, 2018

Little strawberry girl is 25 weeks old today!

She received a book this week, which inspired today's themed shoot.

As much as I am able, I take photos of Carmen. It has helped me to visualize her progress and remember what we have conquered. It is cold and dark in these walls but I try not to let that diminish her light.

Every few weeks, I decorate her room with new pictures. Her providers love it and it kind of gives Carmen a personality. She is not just another baby in a hospital bed. She is Carmen.

Some days my ideas don't work and Carmen is best left to rest. Today I was so excited that Carmen was ready for a few pictures! I was even more excited because she is off all respiratory support as of this morning! The last few days she has looked incredible! Yes, there are still some challenges, but this week we have seen more positive progress and that's what we'll focus on.

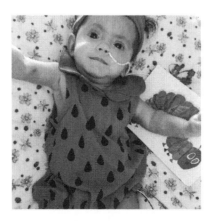

May 21st, 2018 (Morning)

Oh my! Carmen has teeth!

We settled and moved into our new house yesterday. It is so perfect for Carmen! We have been working hard and are all exhausted but I have such a peace that this will be the best place for her.

Come home, baby girl!

May 21st, 2018 (Evening)

Carmen remains in a holding pattern at the hospital awaiting one additional procedure before she is able to come home. This requires considerable patience, as she has had to overcome many obstacles for this surgery to become a reality.

Today the surgeon came to evaluate her and we have decided to move forward with the Nissen Fundoplication and G-tube placement. There are many risks and complications that can occur and this has been a difficult decision to make, but there are no other options.

Carmen is in a good place right now and the surgeon has agreed that if Carmen does not have any other significant issues, the surgery could be set for next Wednesday.

Wednesday also happens to be Carmen's half birthday.

It is a very strange feeling to send her off to yet another surgery with all that it entails, but exciting to think this is her chance!

When Carmen was in the NICU, a nurse told me to always remember the goal is to get home. Home is a beautiful word and it means so much for Carmen to be able to see and be outside of the hospital. I know she will always have difficulties that will bring her back to this place but those first steps out of this building will be enough to endure another six months of this if we must!

We are so thankful to have come this far. Knowing Carmen, she will have many battles ahead, but there is no doubt in my mind that she will be able to overcome them all. God is certainly within her! She CANNOT fail!

Having bought and moved into our first home we have been busy setting up our new place for Carmen. This fresh start has been a huge blessing and we are bursting at the seams to think our baby girl could be joining us here sooner rather than later.

Our new house is in a safe neighborhood convenient to all the important things that will help me be the best mom for my daughters. We will be closer to family for support and I can even walk to pick up all of Carmen's medications.

We have selected a place that is functional for all of her medical equipment and it has wonderful natural light that I just *know* Carmen will love! Come home, baby girl! Please come home!

May 23rd, 2018

Today was a day of many firsts!

While Carmen is back on oxygen, her team is trying out some new ways to help decrease her secretions, which seem to be the culprit for her low oxygen saturation. She is on a nasal spray to reduce the moisture around her mouth and we are discussing the use of Botox injections as well. Medicine is such a blessing!

Carmen also tried food for the first time today! Well, she licked pears and that's at least a start.

Her speech therapist has been working hard to make sure she does not have aversions for the future and has decided to introduce taste. Wow!

Carmen had tummy time and did incredible! I was truly shocked! She did 15 minutes of this and really enjoyed it. I kept wondering where my baby went!

And one of the cutest firsts would have to be her pigtails! Yes, my 6-month old has enough hair for pigtails. Who would have thought?

May 24th, 2018

We celebrated twenty-six weeks of LIFE this evening!

A whopping 10 pounds, 5 ounces and almost 24 inches long!

Carmen had a very special first-time visitor tonight. My friend Lauren and I think she really enjoyed being part of the big girl conversations. As much as Carmen can't see many people, it is always very special for me to have my friends and family come into this room. I know it will only help me in the future to have people by my side that have seen what this life is like. My heart leaps when people are willing to spend their time here with me.

Tonight, Carmen's nurse reminded me again what a miracle this little girl truly is.

Even though I really do think she is a miracle, I sometimes think I have "Mommy bias." Carmen's nurse said that her medical records are just depressing. She reminded me that despite the words written, so much of it doesn't define her! It lists all the very many things she shouldn't do and shouldn't have been able to overcome, and yet she just keeps doing it!

No one told Carmen what she's not supposed to be able to do, so she's just doing them!

May 25th, 2018

Today was my mom's birthday.

It ended up being the perfect excuse to dress the girls in their matching (and stylish) yellow rompers. If there ever were to be a "PICU Style-and-Profile" award, I am positive Carmen would win!

Lately I have just been celebrating everything. I mean, why not? I always thought it best to keep things for special occasions, but now every day that I am upright and breathing is a good enough reason for me!

May 28th, 2018

We are so thankful for inventions like the G-tube and we have gotten to a place where we welcome it with open arms!

Anything that will help our baby girl grow safely and come HOME is fine by us!

We are, however, anxious about the Nissen Fundoplication surgery. In this surgery the top part of her stomach will be wrapped over the bottom of her esophagus to reduce the contents of her stomach from coming back up. Carmen's stomach is very tiny and it will be even smaller once the wrap is complete. It has been important for Carmen to grow so that there is enough space within her frame to be able to do this surgery.

For those wondering, this surgery does not mean she will never be able to eat solids. Actually, it has been suggested that Carmen start with solids and then work backwards to liquids as she grows and matures. She very well might be able to do lots of things and in no way do we want to limit her.

Another myth is that she will not be able to throw up. This is also false, especially if the wrap is able to be as loose as they would prefer. For the first few months, there will be swelling and she will not be able to throw anything up but as time passes, this should pass.

Carmen will stay on continuous feeds for quite some time after her surgery. Her stomach has never been fed and it will need time to adjust. Large, bolus feeds would be painful and harmful for her. This means she will stay hooked up to her feeding pump 24-7 for months, just as she is now.

This little girl has expanded our world 10^{80}! We share our journey because of others who have shared theirs and have helped us tremendously!

This surgery feels very different than her others because we have known about it for so long. This truly could be the big step that points Carmen in the direction of life outside the hospital.

This is no easy surgery and it comes with many possible complications. It was not an easy decision to make but as a team and as a family, we have decided that we have to give her a chance. Living in the hospital is risky and as Carmen grows and thrives, it will only become more difficult.

Wednesday morning she will journey to the operating room once again. We pray that the surgery will be successful and without complication during and after. We pray against infection or bleeding and for no unseen injuries to occur during the procedure. We pray for her pre- and post-op care and for her to once again find the strength and peace needed to overcome this battle.

On Wednesday, May 30th Carmen will be six months old.
God is so faithful.

Tomorrow we will be celebrating her beautiful life and we hope that you celebrate the lives around you as well! Miracles are all around us!

May 29th, 2018

How? How has it been six whole months?

I would be lying if I said it's gone by quickly. I'd be lying if I said I wish I could go back. I'd be lying if I said I could do it all again. As much as I dislike how long Carmen has been in the hospital, I also remember not knowing if Carmen would make it to one month, to the next day, or to the next hour.

It's hard to wake up every day with those kinds of thoughts but as her mother I have a choice. No day is a guarantee for any of us and I'd be a fool not to celebrate the gifts I've been given. This year I read "If your heart is still beating, your mission isn't over yet!" And I truly believe that. For however long your heart is beating, my love, I will be sure to celebrate you and make your life beautiful! Your purpose is clear and I know without a doubt you are changing lives!

This little girl is a masterpiece. She is a light and a force. She is a story and I am her voice.

She is loved deeply and was created in the image of a perfect God. And today we celebrate. We celebrate her life and everyone who has helped us get through day after day, for half a year.

We celebrate the chance of life and the choice of happiness. Happy Half Birthday, sweetie!

Tomorrow will be dark, but I know you will SHINE!

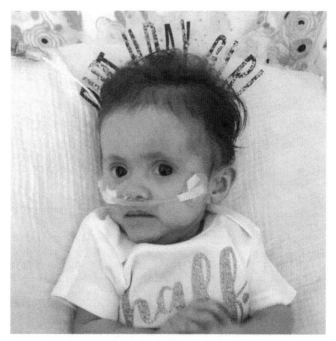

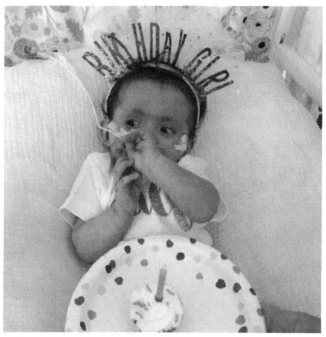

May 30th, 2018 (Morning)

Carmen is in the operating room for her Nissen Fundoplication surgery, G-tube placement and therapeutic Botox injections.

This morning she looked strong and ready! Her entire team is eagerly awaiting the completion of this major hurdle that could bring us much closer to home. Prayers are flowing and I am filled with joy at this time.

Big Poppy came to help send Carmen off to surgery covered with prayers! We made sure to send her in style, with her birthday crown on her head.

You've got this, baby girl!

May 30th, 2018 (Afternoon)

Today I cried when I saw Carmen, but it was different because they were tears of joy!

Carmen did very well during surgery. Everything went smoothly and the surgery could even be accomplished through a laparoscopic procedure! Carmen has a new accessory and even got Botox today!

These next few days will be challenging as we all wait and see what Carmen shows us what she can do! God granted us favor today and we are so thankful! Glory, glory, glory!!

May 30th, 2018 (Evening)

This. Girl. Right. Here.

It feels as if Carmen just had her millionth surgery and the little warrior didn't skip a beat!

I was so worried about today and how she would do and if the surgeon could even attempt what was planned. Everything went off without a hitch! I know things can always surface post-op, but it was such a relief to hear things went smoothly.

I got to go down to the OR and help transfer her back to the PICU. She was still intubated and sedated. That lasted only moments before Carmen showed us she was ready to end her little siesta! She was extubated right away and has already begun weaning her oxygen!

She's been movin' and groovin' ever since! Today Carmen has been referred to as a miracle baby, rockstar, champion, queen, and even a diva!

I have been her audience today. You know, that one crazy person who stands up the whole concert, claps unwaveringly and tells everyone around them, "Hey, I know her!" (That's me, all right!) "Go, Carmen, go!"

May 31st, 2018 (Morning)

Carmen has had a fever post-op and is experiencing tachycardia once again.

Her heart rate is now coming down since receiving some extra fluid. She is still going to have to wait another day or two for feeds but has been receiving IV fluid and some medication through her G-tube.

She ripped out the tube that was to be used for venting through her nose so they are now venting from her G-tube. She has been restless but the morphine seems to be helping.

Right now Carmen is rocking the toga look and all of her other vitals, as well as surgery sites, look good! She is down to 2 liters of O_2 flow.

Mommy and Daddy have been learning a lot and are pumped to learn all that we can to help this little sweetie!

May 31st, 2018 (Evening)

My heart might explode!

Thank you, Jesus, for the best little gift I never knew I wanted! Carmen, you give me life!!

Everyone is pleasantly surprised how well Carmen is doing post-op and the "H" word was even mentioned today! We aren't telling Carmen that, but it is just so refreshing to know there is a light at the end of this tunnel. Carmen has her high beams on all the way!

June

THE "H" WORD

June 2nd, 2018

As I stepped out of the elevator to the 8th floor I overheard a brief conversation:

1st person: "Yea, I saw that too! It said 183 days in the PICU!"
2nd person: (Mumbling something I couldn't hear.)
1st person: "No, really that's what it said." (Deep sigh.)

I knew they were talking about Carmen. I didn't even want to look their way because it was all so depressing. Having read every online story I could find to see how long other babies stayed in the hospital, I would compare our situation and say to myself, "No way we'll be here *that* long! We'll be home long before then." And yet many of those numbers that seemed out of reach are now in the rearview mirror. Today marks 184 consecutive days in the hospital.

However, we did receive some wonderful news today. Not *the* news, but close. Carmen is doing quite well and we are heading in the right direction. While I won't share the full details, I will say that it's probably what you are thinking.

Today, I also heard that there are five new "tiny heart" warriors on the unit. I do not know their conditions or what their numbers will be but I do know the darkness and distress their families are facing right now. I am acquainted with the deep uncertainty they feel and the desperate desire they have to be anywhere but here. I know their capacity to love is intensifying and I know the courage they are realizing they never knew they had. I know they are tired, hungry, lost, and hurt. I don't know where they'll be in 184 days but I know that I will pray that they get there.

As much as my eyes wanted to fill with tears of happiness today, I felt humility instead. I felt a desire not to jump for joy, but to fall on my knees with gratitude for 184 days of life and for eyes to see what God sees. I know that God is just as present with all those other babies as He is with Carmen and for that I am overwhelmed with both awe and gratitude. How great is our God!

Jesus, I have seen your hands and your heart. So today as I stand a bit taller knowing we are one step closer to the door, I pray you show your hands and heart to all the families on this unit today.

June 3rd, 2018 (Afternoon)

No ND-tube. No supplemental oxygen.

Carmen is doing amazingly well on a mixture of Pedialyte and formula administered through the G-tube! She is even having a good hair day and is all dressed up! What a blessing it is to see her face sans tubes!

God IS faithful!

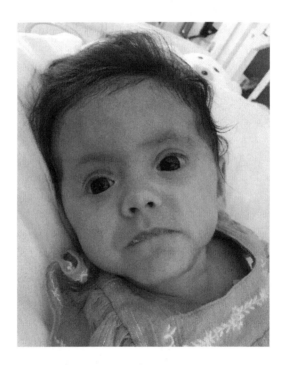

June 3rd, 2018 (Evening)

Now that Carmen does not have a tube in her throat, we have noticed her cry to be a lot louder and she has started making sounds. This is truly a gift because some time ago we were told that Carmen's vocal cords had been stretched in surgery and she may not be able to make any sound. Today, however, she made us laugh so hard!

She's a sassy one!

June 4th, 2018

Carmen is now in intermediate care! Tonight she departed from the ICU and has begun her journey toward the "H" word that we still refuse to say.

While a date has been targeted, we are all remaining flexible since we understand Carmen could always decide on a different date. Also, paperwork and insurance issues could cause delays.

Nate and I, and our entire family, are so excited and can hardly believe that the day is coming near! Today we started all of the preparations and are both overjoyed and overwhelmed by all of the support Inova Children's has provided.

This will be a huge challenge but it is one we are so blessed to be able to take on. Thank you all for surrounding us in love, prayer, and hope! We have been very encouraged and hope this news can be encouraging to you!

June 5th, 2018

Daddy and Mimi have been receiving education on Carmen's care today. They are getting practice administering all of her medications, oxygen, breathing treatments and nutrition. And Carmen is practicing sitting in her car seat for the very first time! She will need to pass a 90-minute car seat challenge fairly soon.

Mommy gets to hang out with Holland today, which is rare but so very special!

I work on Carmen's room whenever I have the chance and even made my own medical binder to stay organized. I also produced this lovely sign for our home!

June 8th, 2018

"She made broken look beautiful and strong
look invincible.
She walked with the Universe on her shoulders
and made it look like a pair of wings."
-Ariana Dancu

Happy twenty-eight weeks, baby! You're
perfect.

June 10th, 2018

Holland, I love you.

I love you for making me slow down, for forcing me to make messes, for making me laugh. I love every ounce of your spirit and the joy you bring others! You are going to be the best big sister for Carmen! God is going to do mighty things through you, my dear!

We have spent the last few days creating a happy home for Carmen to come to. Holland had to test everything out first just to make sure!

She is going to love it!

Name: Carmen Grace Hatcher
Born: November 30th, 2017
@ INOVA Children's Hospital

Medical complexities at discharge include,
but are not limited to:

Pre-mature (34 weeks)
IUGR (growth restriction)
Low Birth weight
Heart Defects (VSD closed with device, reconstructed
Coarctation of the Aorta, ASD. Hypo-plastic BAV- left
side
of heart
Difficult Airway, Difficult intubation.
Kidney (Horseshoe Kidney- Kidney Failure
& Kidney Reflux)
Brain Anomaly Cerebellar vermis hypoplasia
Chylothorax: Thoracic duct ligation
Feeding intolerance. G-Tube- Continuous feeds.
Severe reflux & aspirations- Nissen Fundoplication
completed.
Micrognathia (Jaw)
Vocal cord Paralysis
Insufficient immune system. SCID
Blood clots

*Genetic Anomalies:
Xp deletion, 9q22.2-9q34.3 duplication
Unbalanced translocation.

...All undiagnosed prenatal

June 12th, 2018 (Morning)

Glory, glory, glory!

Today is indeed a good day! In just a few hours Carmen will begin her life outside the 8th floor of the INOVA Fairfax Hospital.

There is no other experience I have ever had that compares with what I feel today.

Leaving the building that saved my daughter's life (and mine) to begin life outside these walls feels… Surreal.

This place was always confusing to me. Every single day was difficult and every single day Carmen had to fight.

Twenty-eight weeks of fighting.

Many days I thought this was just what our lives would be — the driving back-and-forth; the tests; the surgeries. The hospital is our normal. It was her home.

We haven't known any other. And for that I can't fathom what walking out of these doors with my baby will be like.

When I try to envision it I cry because I am afraid and nervous. Will I be able to care for her? Is she really ready? I even weep at the excitement of seeing what she can do beyond her hospital bed. I cry because this is going to be downright difficult every single day and some days I'll wonder if I truly have it in me. I cry because this is familiar and every single thing outside these doors will be new for her and we have no idea what she will do and how she will respond.

I cry because I am proud to be Carmen's Mommy more than just about any other thing. She has taught me to be brave, to fight, to get my hands dirty, to push through every uncomfortable moment and <u>expect bad things not to last forever.</u>

Carmen taught me to refuse to take no for an answer, to trust, and to wait. She has taught me to love hard and fast, to celebrate every tiny victory, to pray unceasingly, and to never, ever give up.

Today when we pack her last hair bow, hug our last incredible caregiver and then walk out of this air-controlled environment into the sun... God receives all the glory.

I think that's why I cry the most. From the beginning we had to trust that God's plan for Carmen was to leave the hospital and that His will would be the most perfect way to glorify Himself. And this included the possibility that Carmen might not come home. God is faithful. Carmen is coming home!

June 12th, 2018 (Night)

Carmen is home.

I honestly couldn't tell you the time we arrived because it has been very chaotic.

Despite six months of planning for this day, we were still overwhelmed with the logistics of the transition.

One of Carmen's care providers rode home with and two nurses assisted as we unpacked numerous boxes of medical equipment. We are still not quite sure where we would like to be, but we are managing.

Tonight is our first night alone with Carmen and we pray she rests easy and finds peace in this new atmosphere. Tomorrow evening we hope to have Holland join us. She is having a great time with GiGi and Big Poppy.

We are home! God blessed us profoundly today!

June 13th, 2018

One of us slept throughout the night while the other barely got a wink having to pinch oneself and play doctor. I'll let you guess who was who.

Carmen successfully made it through her first night at home. Mommy celebrated at 6:30 AM because I handled each and every task, flawlessly! When the sun started peeking out I took a deep breath. Thank you, Jesus! She is HOME!

June 14th, 2018

Despite just how challenging and unrelenting the work has been over the last few days, we are getting it done!

And Carmen is thriving! She is getting three more teeth, which will soon bring us to lucky number seven. She has been rolling to both sides and today we believe she is starting to actually reach out to touch things. She has also found her voice and though the sounds are a bit odd, it is so cute. She certainly has much to say!

Carmen doesn't exactly have a schedule. She is used to being on the hospital regimen with lots of tests and checks throughout the day and then sleeping at night. It's pretty awesome that she sleeps through the night. Her monitors, feeding pump, and medication schedule keep us on our toes, though.

Holland is also going through a tough transition and we are trying to go slow and help to make both girls feel equally cared for and included.

Thank God for our incredible mothers who are making this as manageable as it can be! Nate, you rock! We make a great team!

Carmen qualifies for an extensive amount of home nursing care at this time and we are in the process of managing their assistance as well.

Tomorrow is Carmen's first post-discharge doctor's appointment. I am anxious to take her out of the house with all her "accessories" and am praying for a positive experience.

June 15th, 2018

I sent Nate a video of Carmen smiling today and
he responded, "Did you ever think you would
see this day?"

My initial reaction was that I didn't. But actually,
I think I did. It's what I've hoped and prayed
for. The magnificent thing about God's plan is
that the wonder of this day is greatly magnified
having gone through such a storm. He makes all
things new and ALL things beautiful in His
timing.

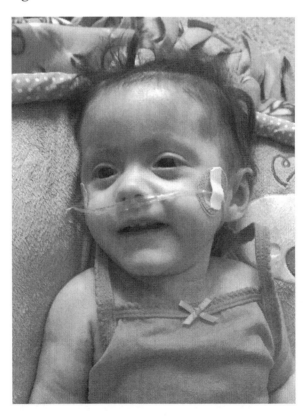

June 17th, 2018

Happy Father's Day!

The day that Carmen's genetic results came back, I called Nate to give him the news.

I was trying not to cry as I told him what the counselors suspected for Carmen's life. After I explained all I could, Nate said, "I am so excited! I hope she has so many needs that she never leaves us and we can just love her forever!"

I lost it! In that moment I knew Nate would indeed be the perfect father for Carmen. I knew what Nate said came from his soul and that he truly meant every word. It almost made perfect sense that God would give Carmen to us because He knew we would love her so much.

This year, Nate and I have spent just about every day and night apart. We have been stretched, challenged, and changed. It has been incredibly difficult. There have been monumental moments, but none of them were fun, romantic, or pretty. They were rough and required lots of work. We are not the same people who married almost five years ago and we are not the same people who brought Holland into the world.

As parents, Nate and I have played every role whether we wanted to or not. You must if you want to get things done.

In the coming days after Carmen's diagnosis I was told time and time again, "The husbands don't stay." I always responded that anyone thinking this would apply to Nate simply doesn't know him. There is no doubt in my mind that Nate wouldn't even consider abandoning the child God entrusted to us no matter how grievous the situation. She is ours and we delight in her and our strong tribe of four.

The days and nights are long, but there is no one else I would rather have by my side; no matter the distance and how rough the road gets. Happy Father's Day to all the dads who don't give up, who work hard and do their best, who love when it's not romantic, and lead when the way is dark.

We love you!

June 19th, 2018 (Afternoon)

Carmen had a great follow-up with her gastroenterologist today!

She has grown so much since leaving the hospital and we are already reducing her calories and rate of her feeds. She is 11 pounds, 13 ounces and today she decided to roll over! It's a skill she has been working on recently but I was surprised how fast she did it, tubes and all!

Carmen's adjusted age is five and a half months, so we are thrilled about this milestone! We are realizing that Carmen's hospital stay made her very independent. This girl rocks herself to sleep and plays with her hair for comfort. In some ways it saddens me to know that she has had to learn how to soothe herself but in other ways I am so pleased because she has learned to be content all on her own. Now we can spend time working on other skills!

June 22nd, 2018 (Morning)

Happy Friday, everyone!

We made it ten days at home and for that we are celebrating! Carmen can't exactly enjoy the sunshine yet, so she creates her own.

We are hoping in the next two weeks Carmen will be able to go outside, weather permitting. If it's too sunny or hot, her heart has to work extra hard. We will be patient and wait for a good day.

She was a perfect 10 on the adorability scale, so you know I just had to take some pictures before she gets vaccinations this morning.

June 22nd, 2018 (Evening)

Today has been a bit odd.

We took Carmen to get vaccines but out of nowhere she spiked a temp of 101.4, so they had to hold off for today. We were sent home to monitor her temp over the next two hours with the plan of heading back to the hospital if it remained. However, she has had no fever since being home. We suspect that Carmen was wearing too many clothes and was under some stress during the check-up, which led to the higher-than-normal numbers.

She is also getting yet another tooth. I know, crazy.

Carmen has actually gained a lot of weight, which is not as great as we would think. She has actually gained too much, too fast and we are now revising her nutrition plan. It's been a day of ups and downs—fever, no fever; too big, not big enough. This girl likes to keep me on my toes. Doesn't she look so grown up?

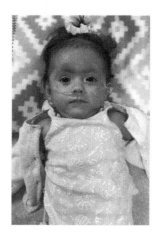

June 23rd, 2018

Carmen laughed for the first time this evening!!!

MiMi, good job! We were all so surprised! I had to run and get Nate out of the shower to witness this. Thank you, Jesus!

The most wonderful thing about this was that she began laughing at the very anticipation of being tickled! I know her therapists will be thrilled with this news!

June 24th, 2018

Today I got in the car to run a few errands, which is something normally so simple yet almost impossible over the past year.

Nate had the girls taken care of so I could spend a few moments alone. Woo-hoo! I almost did a double take at myself in the rearview mirror as I pulled away from our house. I left without that terrible lingering fear. It felt so good to breathe.

Carmen has been home for just 13 days, and yet it seems that those six and a half months in the hospital happened a lifetime ago. When I think of all the effort expended throughout the year to just get to today, I could not account for how we actually made it here. Except, that is… Jesus.

Two minutes into my drive a lady on the radio began speaking about her daughter. She was a girl with disabilities who seemed to have recently passed away. The mom said that even the last day her daughter was on earth, she prayed that God would heal her. That was always her prayer. God eventually took her to Heaven where she would be made new. No pain, no disabilities. The mom said she realized quickly that "God answers our prayers in the most miraculous ways. However, the way in which He answers prayers are different than we want them to go most of the time."

You and I can only see what is directly in front of us in the very moment we are in. That's it. When we pray, our prayer is in the context of what we think would be best either for the present or how we foresee our future.

However, God sees everything. He sees our hearts, our past, our present, and our future. He sees how we interact with those around us and He knows exactly what will be best for us. He doesn't only want the best for our today, but also for next year. He wants what's best for our mind, our body, and, most importantly, our soul.

Just about every testimony I've ever heard has some sort of trial or hardship that ended up being the gateway or stepping stone to meeting Jesus. He cares so much for us that *He would rather break us today in order to help us build a bridge to eternity.*

As I sat in my car for a while, I began to think of all the prayers I've ever uttered. And the tears began.

I thought about Nate, about his family, about my family, about the changes that have occurred over the years. I thought about those who are not part of our circle anymore and the new friends we have been blessed with. I thought about those who have passed and those fighting for their lives this very moment.

I thought about Montenegro, where Nate and I served, and all that it took to get there and back. I thought about everything I've done and those things I didn't finish. I thought about everything my 15-year-old self wanted and the overwhelming joy I now have since Jesus lives within me.

Just about every single prayer I've ever lifted up has been answered. And there are unanswered prayers that I clearly see God's hand moving within.

Carmen being home is an answer to prayer. It does not mean I prayed harder than any other mom who faithfully asked for her child to come home. It does not mean that I was rewarded for being a "good person," and it does not mean all of the trials are behind us. It means that Carmen's story gets to continue in a setting that we are so undeniably grateful for. But this answer to prayer for me is not something I ever want to forget.

Over the past few months many people have heard about Jesus through Carmen's story — in the hospital, in elevators, families I've met online, friends from my past, and even members of our own family. Some have heard of Him for the first time and others have been granted a new spark of His goodness that must be responded to.

I've heard stories of marriages that have held on, and of mothers and children who have decided to forgive one another. I've heard of mercy being practiced and I've seen acts of selflessness that comes from being a faithful servant. I've been able to share the good news of Jesus Christ with more people just this year than on all my mission trips combined. I've prayed more faithfully for complete strangers and have spoken more confidently about God's miracles all because a little girl came into this world with only a fighting chance to survive.

Recall that my prayer for Carmen was always that she would have *a unique gift that would bring Glory to God.*

When I think of my prayer, sometimes it scares me. Most days I feel this prayer has already been answered tenfold. There are very few people I know who have brought the amount of glory to God that Carmen has. Every day that she is here it is not only a miracle but it is proof that God is doing wonderful things in, on, through, and around her.

Every day that we wake up, every minute that we are here, every breath that we take means He is NOT done with us yet.

We all have a story to write or tell. We all have something to be thankful for. This evening I encourage you to take a step no matter where you are on your spiritual journey. It will not be an easy or comfortable path, and at times you won't be able to see one foot in front of the other, but if you step out in faith you will not be alone. You can walk confidently knowing some*One* is with you and helping to get you where you need to go.

June 26th, 2018

The last two days Carmen had three doctors' appointments.

Nate and I are so proud that we were able to take Carmen by ourselves and with Holland in tow, too! It takes a lot of teamwork, patience, and good communication; the whole "teamwork makes the dream work" thing is itself a work in progress, but we're in it to win it!

Yesterday we got the great news that Carmen's lungs are healing well and she is able to discontinue her breathing treatments for the summer and will resume again in September. This is one less thing we have to do for her nightly care!

Carmen's pulmonologist gave permission for her to be off oxygen for segments of the day. While she is awake, alert, comfortable, and if her oxygen saturation stays in the 90s we can start practicing! This is fantastic because right now while Carmen is on oxygen at home, she is confined to an area that's only about six square feet.

The pulmonologist also green-lighted Carmen for some time outside! We are to start in the evening when the temps are cooler and keep her away from small children. This is also a blessed development for the simple reason that being cooped up inside is, well, not so fun!

Today we went to see one of our favorite cardiologists. This was a two-hour appointment and Carmen didn't like it one bit. She screamed for most of the echocardiogram and cried until she fell asleep. I kept thinking she was having flashbacks of the hospital. Poor baby.

At the end of all the testing, there was concern that the same area that was repaired during her original surgery (and balloon dilated since then) is narrowing again. This was discouraging as it hasn't been that long since her last catheterization. I wasn't expecting to hear news of this sort for at least a few more months or even years. As a result, Carmen will have another echocardiogram on July 11th to see if the gradient is greater than today and if an intervention is needed.

Overall, the little warrior princess is doing great! We love having her home even if we do have to bring her to the doctors periodically. We are striving to keep Carmen with us as long as she is comfortable and happy. Honestly, our family just feels complete with her here. Oddly enough, things feel easier since she has been home and we just adore watching our two daughters interact.

June 27th, 2018 (Morning)

When your night nurse didn't show up and your day nurse just called in sick you take it as a sign that God gave you two hands for a reason! I also pray that I grow two more hands before my two-year-old wakes up and gets moving!

June 27th, 2018 (Afternoon)

Yes. This is what we did today.

Now I know why my mom always dressed my sister and I alike! It truly is the cutest thing ever!

June 29th, 2018

Last night was the first (and last) night we had a nurse here. I'd say it went well, except for the part where Carmen's alarm kept going off due to her pulse oximeter (to monitor blood oxygen levels) being incorrectly placed.

After going up and down the staircase in the dark ten times, I ended up falling down the entire flight, landing flat on my face.

Anyway. It's Friday. Whatever that means.

June 30th, 2018 (Afternoon)

Carmen is seven months old!

This is the first monthly update picture not taken in the hospital. Yay! The only thing Carmen cared about during this photo shoot was trying to take her bow off, which she eventually did.

Last night I was so happy. I put Holland to bed and started Carmen's nightly care. It made me so joyful to care for her in so many ways. I thought to myself how there is absolutely nothing I would change. Sure, I wish she didn't have to go through all the pain and procedures, but all in all, I wouldn't change any day we've had so far. She has taught me more in seven months than my 26 years prior. I am so blessed to be her mommy.

I love you, Carmen Grace. You are wonderfully made.

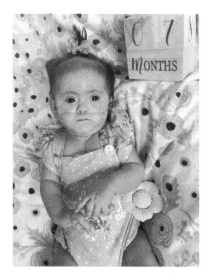

July

FAITHFULLY FREE

July 2nd, 2018

Last night Carmen gave me a few scares.

Her oxygen saturation kept falling and twice her heart rate dropped. I started getting my things in order and preparing in case we had to head to the hospital. The rest of the night was less eventful and today Carmen is yet to have any episodes. Thank the Lord!

This morning our amazing friend and nurse, Nancy, accompanied us to Carmen's neurology appointment, which turned out to be uneventful. Amen! No news is always good news in our case.

I spent the majority of the afternoon on the phone with doctors and social workers. After firing our in-home nursing agency last week, we have been learning so much about the behind-the-scenes work on Carmen's care. It is such a great feeling to check things off my very long list!

This evening I get to finally do what I love. I get to be a mom and love on my girls. We do not know what tomorrow brings, but tonight we are home and we are together.

July 4th, 2018

Happy Independence Day!

Today is Carmen's first official holiday home! It's so crazy to think I was in the hospital two days after Thanksgiving last year and have spent every holiday in that building since. I am so pleased that we can finally celebrate together in the same room!

This morning didn't start off as I had expected. Not going into the details but just imagine a quadruple dose of "mom guilt" on steroids and you get just a taste of how stupid I feel right now. While we have avoided trips to the hospital for more than three weeks, we have certainly had our close calls and this morning was no exception. God is good (even when I am not) and He gives us grace for each day!

It is fitting that we get to celebrate independence together today. Through Christ we *are* independent and SO FREE (John 8:36)!

July 5th, 2018

"Delight yourself in the Lord, and he will give you the desires of your heart." (Psalm 37:4)

I've read this verse many times but tonight I HEARD it for the very first time!

I will start off by saying:
1. I am exhausted.
2. My legs hurt.
3. I am so in love!

This is difficult for me to admit, but I never truly knew what I wanted to be. For the majority of my life if you asked me the golden question, I would have answered "a dancer!" And that's what I was.

But that was fairly short-lived and I never had a solid plan B. Every single thing that I found interesting and hoped could be translated into a livelihood paid little (if anything) or was something I had to pay to do. Frankly, that didn't bother me too much. I really only knew that I wanted to help people and see the world!

I've volunteered, interned at a psych ward, mentored youth, and served as a missionary. In those different scenarios I was always an aide, assistant, or helper. And I was okay with that. I discontinued my college studies in large part because I truly never thought I would get the proper return on the financial investment it would require. I felt I learned better in other environments and I could never settle on a major that didn't make my stomach turn at night.

So what was the desire of my heart?

I think I have previously bundled my heart's desire with those of my brain, body, and wallet.

Over the last five years, God has scraped away the importance that society holds on my decision-making. He has made me uncomfortable in many surroundings in order to make me more comfortable in my own skin. He has stretched me greatly to not only search for His hand at work, but to expect it and participate in what He is doing.

But tonight, as I separate out the desires of JUST my heart, I think of the many prayers I've offered.

I've prayed to "see" Christ. To see what He sees. To have a voice for Him. To bring glory to Him. To bring others to Him. To love ferociously and be a part of advancing His kingdom in any way I am able.

Every time I look into my children's eyes, I see God. I see Him in their bodies, which were created perfectly by Him. I see His hands when I care for them. I see His heart when my eyes are open to the many people who often feel invisible. I see so clearly how He has orchestrated each and every moment of my life to bring me to this season.

So as I sit here listening to the rather loud hum of the oxygen machine (and poised to jump at any beep) with my unwashed hair and grumbling stomach, I smile.

260

I smile because my God isn't one who focuses on my comfort or even my physical condition. While I know He cares for these things, I know He has other more profound purposes. My heavenly Father listens intently to my prayers; prayers that were never for clean hair or a quiet home. He is focused on my heart. And my heart is completely full!

July 6th, 2018

Carmen got to meet the final member of our immediate family today!

Aunt Bethany is here for the week!

July 9th, 2018

Every single day that I gaze upon this growing body, which is covered in scars, I am reminded of a great hope.

While I wish I could have taken each of these twelve scars myself, I know that every mark has a purpose and every blemish shows more than just pain and brokenness. To me, these scars are lines pointing straight to a healing God who knew Carmen would wear them as beautiful works of art and proof that miracles happen.

July 10th, 2018

Today marks one month since Carmen was discharged from her almost seven-month stay in the PICU.

It is incredible to me that we made it an entire month with very few dangerous moments.

There were a few things that were extremely important to me once she got home. One was having family pictures taken of the four of us that were not in a hospital setting. I planned for these photos to be taken before her next cardiologist appointment just in case they decide she needs to be admitted. And we all know how long Carmen likes to stay in the hospital!

Carmen was able to disconnect from her feeds, oxygen and constant monitoring for a brief time as these shots were taken in and around our home. It was such a fun evening filled with smiles and love!

Our wedding photographer, Hannah, captured these images for us. I know I will treasure them forever.

Pictures have always been important to me. They show where we've been and have helped me see growth that sometimes is difficult to notice. Pictures help me embrace both the good and the bad. Enjoy!

July 12th, 2018 (Afternoon)

Two weeks ago, Carmen had a follow-up visit with her cardiologist.

The echocardiogram taken during the appointment revealed that there was narrowing in her aortic valve, which is both the same spot where her original surgery took place and right where she needed balloon dilation just two months ago. The gradient was obvious but not very concerning, so we decided to have another follow-up about two weeks later, which was yesterday. A visit to the catheterization lab was tentatively scheduled for July 24th in the event the narrowing has worsened.

During yesterday's visit we learned that the narrowing was more obvious. This was not a huge surprise to me because the last two days Carmen has desaturated more and her gagging has been worse. We've had to increase Carmen's oxygen levels a bit, which I hated to admit.

Last night her team discussed plans and have decided to go forward with another balloon dilation of her valve. Because Carmen is outpatient, the soonest this procedure can be done is July 24th. However, we have all prepared and all agree that Carmen should most likely not wait until then for this to occur. The other option is to admit her to the hospital where there would be more flexibility on receiving this procedure.

For now, we have decided to keep Carmen home and feel we can care for her during this time as she is stable, happy, and growing. If there are any other changes, Carmen will be admitted back to INOVA Children's Hospital.

God has always had Carmen in the palm of His hand, and today is no different. We do pray for discernment and appropriate timing when it comes to intervening.

Carmen is currently napping right next to her wonderful aunt Bethany and she has given some of the biggest smiles today!

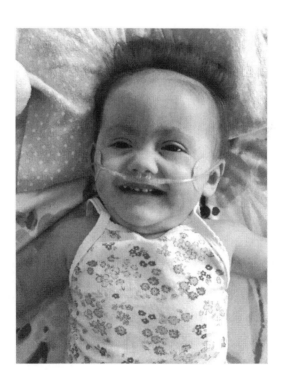

July 12th, 2018 (Evening)

Guess what? I love Jesus! And Carmen! As much as I worried throughout today, Carmen didn't.

Carmen doesn't know half of what she faces and she doesn't know the things "they" say she won't be able to do. And obviously she doesn't care! This munchkin rolled over yet again!

She lifted her head both ways with her legs in a tiny crawling motion! She has close to zero muscle tone in her chest and back, but she is trying as hard as she can!

I just love that when I focus on the things I think are hopeless or impossible, or even just difficult, God is consistent. I love that God shows us how we are supposed to be as little children with our faith.

A child's trust is so innocent and without hesitation. To me, Carmen shows me to be just as I am. I am a daughter of the King who created every star in the sky, the one who gives all living things sufficient breath each minute.

Who am I to worry about tomorrow?

"Do not be anxious about anything, but in every situation, by prayer and petition, with thanksgiving, present your requests to God. And the peace of God, which transcends all understanding, will guard your hearts and your minds in Christ Jesus." (Phil. 4:6-7)

July 13th, 2018 (Late evening)

Carmen has been very irritable for 24 hours now and her stomach is hard and swollen.

We have tried every possible way to troubleshoot her G-tube and venting with no success. We are currently on our way to the ER at INOVA Children's Hospital as advised by her doctor.

July 14th, 2018 (Middle of the night)

No improvement with Carmen's stomach. We believe it has actually worsened. The x-ray of her lungs came back clear and the image of her abdomen shows that it is covered in gas bubbles. Her white blood cell count is elevated so they believe she may have a virus of some sort that is causing motility issues. She was sent to ultrasound around 2:45 AM and three different techs attempted to find her appendix with no success.

Once admitted to intermediate care (IMC), the nurses tried to vent her using three techniques without success. We are trying to be patient as we wait to see if Carmen can clear the assumed blockage on her own and also have a look at what the rest of her blood work shows.

Carmen is exhausted but extremely uncomfortable. She is very hungry and has been attempting to eat her IV tubes. She has not had appropriate rest over the past 36. Her heart rate is up to 224 at the moment and she is hard to calm down.

Praying for some relief soon.

July 14th, 2018 (Morning)

Baby girl has been rushed to admission in the PICU.

She is being treated for distended stomach, the cause of which is yet to be determined. She is also having what we believe are seizures or similar events. Specialists are now performing an EEG (electroencephalogram), which measures brain activity utilizing an array of electrodes attached to the scalp.

Her temperature has risen to 105 and her heart rate has stayed above 230 for hours on end. Carmen is currently in the intensive care unit and is being cared for by a large team of doctors. The plan is to intubate her as it is thought that she will be very tired and end up needing more support as the day goes on.

Her entire body is swollen and she is very out of it. There is belief that Carmen could have a virus or infection that has caused all of this. Never have I seen my baby in such poor health.

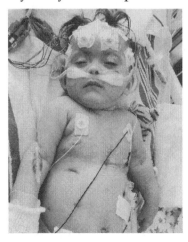

July 14th, 2018 (Afternoon)

GREAT is thy faithfulness! His mercies are new EVERY single morning! (Lamentations 3:22-23)

This illness is new to us, unknown, and seems impossible but GOD has gone before us and nothing surprises Him. Our faith will stand firm and on this very rock we proclaim His glory!

Carmen Grace is a child of a mighty Savior who has given her the purpose of enduring many things to build His kingdom. She challenges doctors to think of things they have never seen and inspires all of us to push through the seemingly impossible. I love you, Carmen Grace! Your whole family is aching for your recovery. We are right here, baby girl!

July 15th, 2018 (Morning)

Carmen took a rapid decline and is now intubated and medically paralyzed.

Still no plan. Please pray for appropriate intervention!

July 15th, 2018 (Afternoon)

Clinically, Carmen is at the end of what can be done for her.

Surgery has agreed to take her to the OR and the team is getting ready to transport her. They still do not know if they will find anything or even what they *could* find. The swelling is so severe that we have no choice but to see what is going on inside. The next few days will be extremely difficult for Carmen as they explore and clear everything.

She will have to go to the OR every 48 hours. Please pray for an answer to this unknown illness!

God, Carmen is your child!

July 15th, 2018 (Evening)

We have no answers, but Carmen is up from the OR.

We hope that in the next few days the culprit emerges and shows its hideous face.

Currently, Carmen's intestines are being purposely kept outside her body in what is called a silo—a clear bag that allows the intestines and other organs to bulge without pressuring the heart and lungs. This allows for her intestines to be monitored for discoloration that could help identify the illness. Having witnessed Carmen enduring multiple open-heart surgeries, I thought I had seen it all. I was wrong. This is the most horrifying thing I have ever witnessed.

I wish something became obvious in the OR and was able to be remedied but we must wait on God's perfect timing.

July 16th, 2018

Last night I slept in the ICU.

It was quiet... too quiet. I am so accustomed to the humming, beeping, and gentle whirring of life-sustaining devices and last night there was hardly any.

Carmen is very sedated. Because of her extensive history with narcotics, she requires very high doses to keep her comfortable. While I cannot share a picture of Carmen at this time, please know my heart is breaking to see her this way. The smell is something I will most likely never forget and I know this image will haunt me for years to come.

Today, two of Carmen's surgeons came to evaluate her intestines and have deemed them "unwell." Although surgery did not yield what could lead to a permanent fix, space was created that allows increased blood flow to her other organs. This was the only option.

Tomorrow Carmen will go back to the OR in order to begin determining which parts of her bowel are healthy enough to keep and what must be removed. This will be a very deliberate process that we have been told will take approximately two weeks. Hearing this news makes me sick to my stomach. There is no part of me that thinks I will be able to get through weeks of this.

That said, Carmen will be in the PICU for a long time. We cannot anticipate how long, since we know Carmen marches to the beat of her own drum. It tears my heart apart to know that, yet again, I will not be able to hold my baby, to comfort her, to have her with me for such a long time.

Today 25 different doctors discussed Carmen's case and still have no answer as to why this happened.
A few nursing students were working alongside her intensive care nurses today and were told, "This is Carmen. Whatever you learned in school doesn't really apply to her. She does what she wants."

Baby girl, I'm not sure why God has given you so many mountains to move, but there is no doubt that you will move each one of them for His glory.

I may cry and scream and think it's the end but, with God's help, please know I will always get back up and fight for you! You are, first and foremost, His! I love you.

July 17th, 2018 (Afternoon)

Is it too much? Is this doing more good than bad? Is the suffering too great? Has all hope vanished?

I would be lying if I didn't admit to considering these questions. And those who have reached out to me and asked if I have pondered these things... Yes. A million times, yes.

The battle that I fight is absolute torment but it is different than the battle Carmen fights. As much as I have attempted to articulate her story, it is *hers*. The moments I have looked at her and thought (even knew) it was the end... Well, it wasn't. Who am I to say she is done fighting? Who am I to say this is too much? Who am I to give up?

I know the words God spoke to me as clear as day. He said, **"I will bless you for your faithfulness."** He did not say what the blessing would be but I know the blessings that God gives are greater than any blessing I could ever desire for myself. I will not be a fool and think all my wishes will be granted if I beg Him to save her. She is already His, whether that's on earth or in heaven. There is no difference. She is His.

 "If we live, we live for the Lord; and if we die, we die for the Lord. So, whether we live or die, we belong to the Lord. For this very reason, Christ died and returned to life so that he might be the Lord of both the dead and the living." (Romans 14:8-9)

The sufferings are great. I HATE watching this. And I know God HATES this more. Carmen was put on earth to bring glory to God. The God who in ALL things works for the good of those who love Him and are called according to His purpose (Romans 8:28). ALL things! Not just the pretty things, the good songs, the perfect services, the grand gestures, the beautiful, the known, the easy, but ALL things.

Sitting in this hospital room, I watch the faces of those who care for Carmen transform into hearts that have to look for hope. This reassures me that God is working. These doctors and nurses love Carmen. She is family here and she was specifically picked to be here.

Carmen will go back for another surgery today at 11:30 AM. This is a procedure rife with mystery. Not only can we not anticipate the outcome but the purpose of this major undertaking is to fix an unknown defect. But none of this is mysterious to the Lord and in that truth we do our best to find peace.

The writer of Hebrews encourages readers to "...run with perseverance the race marked out for us, fixing our eyes on Jesus, the pioneer and perfecter of faith. For the joy set before him he endured the cross, scorning its shame, and sat down at the right hand of the throne of God. Consider him who endured such opposition from sinners, so that you will not grow weary and lose heart." (Hebrews 12:1-3)

The sufferings are great, but the reward is greater. Whether God decides to keep Carmen here on earth or to bring her to heaven is up to Him. It's not up to me and it's not up to the doctors.

Father, we pray your will be done. We pray against evil and pain and confusion. We pray you receive the glory! And, Father, we pray expectantly. You will bless us all for our faithfulness.

Thank you, Jesus, for this baby girl. Thank you for every second I've held her and every second I've had to stand next to her knowing I have nothing else to give. Thank you for the extravagant hope I have that helps me just stand here and wait. Thank you for making this situation one we can't explain, because I can only look to you.

Thank you for making both Carmen and me strong.

July 17th, 2018 (Late Afternoon)

Carmen is in the OR now.

We have been told that any sections of her bowel determined to be dead will be removed. If the entire bowel is deemed dead, they will leave it in and wait to see if anything changes. If the latter is found to be the case and nothing were to improve then there would be close to no other options on the table for Carmen.

I am numb writing this. Lord, we need you!

July 17th, 2018 (Evening)

Dear family and friends,

I apologize for using this platform to share this update. Nate and I are not able to speak about today yet, and it is easier for me to share this way. Out of respect for my family, do not tell me what you would do or what you have done. Nate and I are not making any decisions at this time and are fully relying on God to direct these steps clearly and in His timing.

We love you all and have been overwhelmed by your prayers and support today. As much as I do not want to write this, each of you have played a role in Carmen's story and we are grateful for your faithfulness to her and us. We do not want her story to end.

Carmen came up from the OR in just one hour. I knew it was too fast. When she was brought into the room my mom and I both held our breath as it was clearly noticeable that the silo holding her intestines was gone. I knew what that meant. The next ten minutes, which seemed like ten years, my mom cried and pleaded. I couldn't look at her as she screamed. I grabbed Carmen's hand and laid my head at her side. I heard nothing. I felt nothing. I was nothing.

The surgeon came in and began talking. I could barely lift my head.

The surgeon said, "Ninety percent of her bowel was dead and we had to remove it. She has 20 centimeters of healthy bowel at this moment and we have three options. One, we do nothing and keep her comfortable until she passes. Two, we close her stomach and keep her comfortable until she passes. And three, we wait until Thursday to see if this 20 cm of bowel is still healthy and attempt to hook it up appropriately and then close her stomach. She will be fed TPN (through her veins) and the road will be very rough, if it works."

Nate walked in just in time for the surgeon to repeat everything. I don't think I heard it either time. We were left alone in the room with just our tears and a decision to make.

Nate got a text message and showed my mom. She began crying again. My grandma Barbara had passed away while Carmen was in the OR. I began crying and then grabbed my mom's hand and said, "I think Grandma left so that Carmen can have a chance! We have to give her a chance!"

I have no idea what this means and we all feel sick and without words. Our bodies are numb and broken. I wish I could throw myself into a brick wall a million times, but we have to be strong. It's not over, baby girl. There is still a speck of a chance and we are going to let you fight!

God, I don't know what you are doing, but we trust you.

July 18th, 2018

Nate and I chose the third option.

We chose to try and give her a chance. We held her hands and asked her to give us some sign that this is what we should do. We met tirelessly with doctors and prayed harder than we've ever prayed before.

We knew we couldn't decide to just let her pass. It was not our decision to make.

Many doctors came to warn us and we looked away and knew God could do the seemingly impossible. We believed and we so wanted you to be the one — the one that miracles were manifested in. And, baby, you are.

Last night, she told us multiple times that this life isn't what she wanted. Twice she stopped breathing and, in all honesty, looking down at her we could already feel as if she had half descended. Our baby girl...

Her cardiologist, Dr. T., whom Nate and I respect immensely, came to speak with us. He has always given Carmen all that he had and has been right by our side from the beginning.

As he and I each sat across Carmen's bed he grabbed my hand.

He explained that we have to know that he is the most optimistic guy in the world. He made clear that he knows just how strong and resilient Carmen is and that he was convinced that we would be great parents to her no matter what. He also explained that there was no decision for Nate and I to make.

Simply hooking up the healthy remainder of her intestines to her colon wouldn't fix anything for her. Because of Carmen's blood clots, there would be no access left for a central IV for her to be able to receive TPN. And in a matter of days, maybe a week, she would likely die of infection or malnutrition—without dignity and in great pain.

I could barely look him in the eye as I felt my whole body give up. Dr. T. left the room and Nate and I prayed.

Nate, through streaming tears, called out to the Lord, "God, from the beginning you have spoken clearly to Sydney! We need to hear you now!"

Almost instantly my tense shoulders fell as I heard…

"It is not this world that matters, God will bless you for your faithfulness in Heaven."

I cried uncontrollably because I knew it was time. The battle was over. My baby girl was going to heaven. I cried even harder because God answered our prayer and it was as if my entire body was charged, covered, and secured. I would see her again. I would see her in heaven. Like no mother should ever have to do, I planned my daughter's final day on earth.

We called our family and told them to meet us at the hospital in the morning. We asked Nate's father to help us dedicate her to the Lord and lead in Holy Communion. I packed a beautiful dress from my childhood to clothe her in and tried to embrace every emotion. Our nurses banded together and made it possible for us to sleep beside our daughter one final night.

And then I chose to celebrate.

July 19th, 2018

Carmen Grace,

You were one thousand miracles wrapped into one tiny body.

You showed us the most joy in the most desperate of places. When we looked into your eyes we saw a love that only Jesus can give. You gave us hearts for the broken and spirits that can conquer all things, including death.

Carmen, from the beginning you beat every odd to come into this world and every day you challenged the impossible. You gave us purpose. You redefined our family. And above all, you gave God all the glory.

Mommy and Daddy are so proud of you! The best little sister, the biggest warrior, and the one that inspires us to be living, breathing testimonies to your strength.

You showed us the gospel in true form. You pointed toward the way for the lost to be found.

Our goal was for you to come home, baby, and now you have the most beautiful home ever. You may be far from us, little love, but your story is far from over.

Thank you for the best 232 days of our lives. God bless you, Princess Carmen. We will always stay **Carmen Strong**.

Love

Mommy, Daddy & Holland

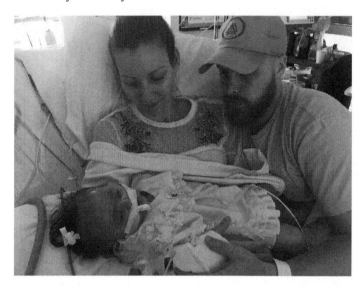

July 23rd, 2018

The first few days I didn't allow myself to write. It was hard and painful; the most raw thing I've ever done. My baby passed away in my arms. I held her body until she reached heaven.

No one should ever have to do that. But I did. And if it had to happen, there is no other way I would have wanted it to be.

It was beautiful. The morning of her passing, our family gathered around her. We dedicated her to the Lord, something I've always wanted to do. We observed Communion and sang "Amazing Grace." It was very fitting.

Holland came to say goodbye to her sister. She innocently told her to wake up and said, "I miss you." We have it recorded and I know one day even Holland will be thankful that she got to say goodbye to her little sister in her own special way.

Carmen was in a dress I wore as a baby and sported a small white bow in her hair. Music played softly and Daddy wrapped his arms around us both. There was pain but even more peace.

Slowly the tubes were taken out and the monitoring stopped. The medications were increased and for an hour I clung to my daughter.

My stomach churned. I knew she would be better off. I knew it was time. I knew it was God's will.

Carmen fought hard her entire life.

Last week we knew the fight was over. One of the most difficult things was looking into the eyes of doctors who had cared for Carmen as if she were their own child — the ones who sustained her and never gave up on her — and see their eyes fade as they truly had nothing left to offer. It was painful to know that if there were even the slightest chance, they would have thrown themselves into the effort. But the simple fact of the matter was that every option had been exhausted. My baby was leaving us.

What kind of life is seven and a half months?

I'll tell you. It was passionate. It was emotional. It was devastating and tragic and true. It was beautiful and it was...*enough*.

From the beginning I felt the need to share Carmen's story. Every time I shared it, I would ask myself, "Why are you doing this?" But I knew I had to.

I made a grand effort every single day to be in Carmen's hospital room. And I can count the days on two hands that I couldn't be there.

When I was there, I was seen as the "crazy" mother — the one who would decorate an ICU room like a nursery, do bi-weekly photo shoots, and go to elaborate lengths to grant at least some ounce of normalcy to her daughter's life. I was the one attempting to make a celebration out of any- and everything (e.g., First-day-to-wear-a-shirt Day, First-time-in-a-stroller Day, etc.).

I had no idea why I was doing these things, but now I do. As her mom, I have great peace in that I will never say, "I wish I had spent more time with her. I wish I had done this or that for her. I wish her life had been more joyful."

Given the circumstances, Carmen's life was the most joyous it could have possibly been and she brought a tremendous amount of gladness to everyone and anyone she met, whether it was in person or from afar.

We are all given a purpose in life and Carmen accomplished hers in just seven and a half months.

Tomorrow is Carmen's funeral. I will do what I have always done for Carmen — celebrate her.

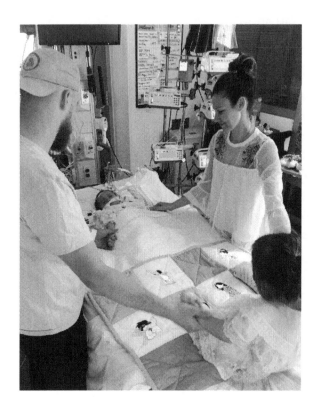

July 24th, 2018

Carmen,

Today more than 900 people came to your Celebration of Life service!

Five people were baptized and many heard the gospel.

It was the most beautiful service I've ever seen.

You were honored, baby girl. I miss you.

We did a butterfly release at our home for you. Holland really enjoyed it. I hope she never forgets you.

July 25th, 2018

This morning I woke up to a home covered in bouquets, each more lovely than the next.

I knew exactly what I wanted to do with them. So my friends and family helped me deliver two cars full of flowers to the Fairfax Hospital PICU on the 8th floor, which was Carmen's prior home. They are so much more beautiful there.

I got to see many of Carmen's doctors and nurses and I was so happy to be there. It's where I wanted to be. And it's where I will continue to visit.

Today I haven't cried at all. Yesterday I cried once. The day before that, once. And the day before that, once. The day I planned Carmen's funeral, once.

This may sound odd, but I can honestly say that last week has been the easiest week I have had in the past year.

When I stop to think about it, there are a number of reasons but it's not very complicated.

First of all, I have grieved every single day since Carmen's birth in light of the fact that we always knew her death was not only a possibility, but very likely. Additionally, her condition was so mysterious that being grief-stricken over the unknowns was as much a reality as the angst we experienced over what we knew was an uphill battle.

294

I grieved bringing her home. I grieved being a mommy to a newborn. I grieved every holiday she was away from us and every second she was missing. I grieved sending her on the bus to her first day of school and I grieved her sweet 16. I grieved planning her wedding and I grieved alongside her knowing she would never be a mommy herself. I have grieved these and other things over and over for the past seven months.

Every day we feared her death. Every night I slept with my phone in my hand waiting for *that* call. I planned every aspect of my life around the possibility of her not being there anymore. I dressed dark and I saw dark and I was dark. The absolute worst-case scenario was always death. And death happened.

But, thank the Lord, I did more than grieve.

I learned to celebrate! I learned to survive and to stand. I learned to seize every single moment Carmen had and did my best to make the best of them. I gave my all.

I think this week was easy for me because every day of her life I didn't wait for perfection. I jumped into the pain and tried to paint it. I stared death in the face day after day and made it known it couldn't rip the smile off my face, even though I thought it eventually would.

For seven and a half months I was a mother to a dying baby. Then her day came and the breath I was holding onto for those months was taken from me. I not only stared at death but held it. I smelled it, was wrapped in it, and spoke to it.

I conquered death. Carmen conquered death.

The worst thing doesn't clutch me anymore. It doesn't hover over me and linger and press into my bones. It doesn't frighten me.
I have an unshakable sense of joy because my baby girl is in heaven. God gave her to me to show me every single thing in this world. He gave her to me so that my heart would grow, my eyes would see, and my fears would be wiped away. Death has no power over me.

"Oh death, where is your victory? Oh death, where is your sting?" (1 Corinthians 15:55)

So here I am picking up the pieces of this beautiful disaster that was Carmen's life, and here I will paint them as beautifully as my earthly hands are able. And here I will live my life to honor her and the One who gave her to me. And here I will promise to tell her story. And here I will promise to not fear anymore.

And here I will raise your soul above the clouds. My new heart is full of life! My body is free from fear of the worst. Loved. More than I ever imagined.

The God of heaven and earth is the same; He never changes.

Thank you to all the hundreds of people who came to celebrate Carmen Grace's life yesterday! Thank you for celebrating her life along with the five people who were baptized and the countless others who now, because of Christ and God's story in Carmen's life, will conquer death as well. God bless you all.

July 26th, 2018

I have tried to be as open and honest with Holland as I feel is appropriate.

She understands far more than I assumed she would about Carmen's life. We decided to include her in Carmen's passing and attempted to make it a peaceful celebration.

Holland is thriving and has a sensitivity to things that is beyond her years. Today we even brought her to pick out an urn. Never did I think I would put that sentence together.

I know that many children prayed for Carmen over these last months. It has been on my heart to try and do something for the parents that will have to explain to their children that Carmen is no longer with us just as I have to do with Holland.

Tonight I received this letter from a friend. It highlights how the most difficult things for adults to do may be simplistic and innocent in a child's mind. There is no right or wrong way to deal with this, but this gave me great peace tonight and I wanted to share these profound words.

Dear Nate and Sydney,

Our family has faithfully prayed and continues to pray for you and your family. Sofia Grace, our 3½-year-old consistently prayed for baby Carmen. She would always ask to see pictures and videos of Carmen; she could never get enough. She would regularly ask how Carmen was doing. When Carmen left the hospital and was able to go home, Sofia was so excited and immediately asked when we could go visit in order to play. I explained to her that baby Carmen wasn't ready for play dates just yet. Sofia was aware that Carmen had returned to the hospital.

The past few days Kelly and I struggled with how we should or even if we would share with Sofia that Carmen went to heaven. We basically decided to not say anything. Last night—July 25, 2018—while I was saying our nightly prayers with the girls, this conversation occurred.

Sofia: "...and, dear God, we pray for baby Carmen. Mommy, is baby Carmen home yet?"

Me: (Long silent pause.)

Sofia: "Mommy, where is baby Carmen?"

Me: "Oh baby, baby Carmen is home with Jesus."

Sofia: "Oh yes! That's good. She is so beautiful."

Me: (mind blown) "Yes, she is beautiful."

Sofia: "Mommy, can I see a picture of Carmen with Jesus?"

Me: "Not right now, baby, but one day. One very special day you will get to see and meet Carmen and Jesus."

Sofia: "OK, that sounds good."

I pray sharing this with you will continue to be a beautiful reminder of what an amazing, purposeful and impactful life Carmen had. Thank you for sharing her with us.

We love you. #alwayscarmenstrong.

July 29th, 2018

Today my friend brought over the most beautiful box. Inside was a custom dress and coral sweater that was designed for Carmen to wear if we decided to bury her. Her passing was quicker than we imagined and an open casket became less of an option. The dress is stunning. It was made and wrapped with love and perfect intentions. But its timing and circumstances just didn't allow for its full beauty to be displayed…just yet, that is.

Tonight another dear friend helped me go through the girls' room and pick out everything that was intended for Carmen. Some things were previously Holland's; others were gifts especially for her. There were shoes and bows and outfits for special occasions. There were her first swimsuit, snowsuit, and everything in between. I came across the outfit I selected as her "going home outfit" back in November, a pale pink sweater set with buttons. Never worn.

We packed bedding and gear and toys. We separated socks and diaper covers and removed hangers that are now too small for Holland's "big girl" clothes. With each item an anticipated memory faded. I never knew you could have memories from the future but I think I've made up a thousand by now.

I'm not sad, though.

Let me to rephrase that.

I'm not sad. Though I had wished for two girls close in age, just like my sister and me…and I had wanted them to play together and grow together and be by each other's side. Though I had seen them drawing while sitting on a two-chaired toddler table in my mind…

Though I had craved to witness Holland care for her baby sister with that pride in her eyes… And though I had anticipated Carmen looking up to her sister and copying her every move... That's not what God saw.

As much as I tried to look past every challenge that was Carmen's life, the Lord decided to bring her to be with Him.
And I'm not sad.

She is free. I am free.

I am not free from the aches of a grieving mother who just lost her baby. I am not free of the worry that consumes my dreams that Holland might be taken too. I am not free from those hoped-for memories that haunt me every time I see two sisters playing. I am not free from having to bite my tongue every time I hear a parent complain about their child. I am not free from exhaustion of trying to figure out how I feel. I am not free from this life. But…

I *am* <u>free</u> from every single thing that ever held me back. I am free from the lies Satan spoke to me all my life. I am free from the excuses I used to make as to why I couldn't do, go, and be…I am free from death.

I fully expected this journey to break every piece of me and I stand here today confused as to why it didn't. I can smile and laugh and think. I have peace and joy and passion—an unrelenting passion that is unexplainable but absolutely undeniable. This passion roars like a lion and consumes like an uncontrollable fire.

I have a second chance at life. That's how I feel.

I feel like I died and came back to life. I feel as if my clock has been reset and my mind has been renewed. My purpose has been clarified and I feel like I have experienced the gospel in all of its fullness—the endurance, the suffering, the waiting for hope, the joy, the peace, and the love.

Carmen showed me who Jesus really is. She showed me both heaven and earth. Her suffering was NOT in vain. Her pain was real but purposed. Her life was short, but worth it.

I saw two sisters playing dolls, all dressed up on Christmas morning.

God saw hundreds of faithless, hurting, lukewarm people needing to see a little girl fight for her life. God saw a community who would rally beside her, whose prayer life would explode and touch lives around the world. God saw families needing to be reminded of His blessings, marriages needing to be mended, people desperate to realize their purpose and passion.

He saw a husband and wife who had a heart for missions, who felt stuck and didn't know they could help anymore. He saw a church that needed revival. He saw an opportunity to bring hundreds, perhaps thousands, to Him through a tiny baby girl.

I saw my two girls waiting together at the bus stop. God saw His children waiting at the gates of heaven.

I am not sad.

Goodnight Prayer

Father God,
Thank you for today.
Thank you for Holland & Carmen & our
wonderful family.
Protect them while they are sleeping,
on earth and in heaven.
Amen

The First Three

Months of Forever

August 9th, 2018

Sometimes I see the look and feel the pause of uncertainty when I talk about heaven. I see the words in their minds that seem to spell out how genuinely they are sorry for me and I feel their lingering hand on my shoulder that screams, "I don't know how you're doing this!"

Frankly, it's unhelpful.

Heaven isn't just a coping mechanism I am using to lessen the hurt of missing Carmen. And neither is it just a means of getting me through the days until I die as well.

I didn't *lose* my baby. Because Jesus Christ rose from the dead, which validates what He said, I know *exactly* where she is.

"Do not let your hearts be troubled. You believe in God; believe also in me. My Father's house has many rooms; if that were not so, would I have told you that I am going there to prepare a place for you? And if I go and prepare a place for you, I will come back and take you to be with me that you also may be where I am." (John 14:1-3)

I am certain that I will see her again. That's how I get out of bed every morning. That's how I get dressed, make breakfast, and go on with my day. That's how I take care of my two-year-old and keep moving forward.

I have to add that since she was called home I have more passion, more desire, more known worth, more color, and more love, too!

But heaven is more than all of this. Heaven has been a real place to me since I was 21. It has been a wonder and it has been foreign. I had never had such a personal relationship with someone who had been there until now, but in just the last five months three of my family members have passed.

People die every single day. There, I said it. We all know this and we all think it will never happen to us. But dying is just about the only thing that one human can bank on!

Of the friends who are in my inner circle now, HALF of them have a child in heaven. Half!

Death is now less of a mystery and doesn't frighten me. I always knew Carmen would pass. I didn't know when, but I knew. God protected me and gave me the wisdom to plan. He also gave me a way to see her again — heaven.

For those who have questioned me on how I could believe in such a place, and about how I could believe in a God that would allow my daughter to suffer and take her from me so quickly and so tragically… It's actually quite simple. Carmen was a miracle (much like you and me) who was granted a specific purpose. The miracle we wanted was for healing, perfection, and life! But we wanted it on *our* terms.

God created the universe in perfection. He created everything on earth in perfect working order, including man. He created all life! But man wanted more. And that desire for more led to the rebellion that led to the Fall, which separated man from God.

Everything was broken and in need of healing. Enter Jesus.

He came as "...the way, the truth and the life (John 14:6)..." to make it possible for us to be reconnected to and in relationship with God. Jesus made the ultimate sacrifice on our behalf and we have the freedom to trust, accept, and follow Him or go our own way. That's it — faith or no faith.

We have the freedom to decide to be our own god (how's that working out?) or put our trust in and pledge allegiance to the Creator that demonstrated an extravagant love for us by writing Himself into our story.

So Carmen died. But Carmen's life was a miracle.

She came to show many people that God is real, that He is in control, that He is able, and that He will give us strength.
She came to pose the questions: What will you choose?

Will you go to heaven where you will experience absolute perfection and live eternally as the person you were really meant to be or will you be lost forever?

Please don't feel bad for me. I don't need your tears. My daughter is in the very presence of the One who sacrificed Himself to save her and is

310

experiencing what true life is. My tears are reserved for those who will not meet us there.

August 19th, 2018

Sometimes I wonder why God allowed me to go through such trying times. I wonder why I almost drowned. I wonder selfishly, "Why me?" I wonder what life would have been like without all the pain and the sickness and the brokenness. I wonder what I would be like if I never saw the darkness. And then I smile.

And that's because when I look in the mirror I don't see a scared little girl who thinks she might know what she wants—a girl who halfheartedly raises her hands before the Lord and doubts her beliefs.

The King of the universe calls me His daughter. He knew what He wanted me to do and see. He knew I could be strong and He knew the war was bigger than what my eyes would see. He knew I would rise above and shout His name before mine. He knew I would give it all up for His glory. He knew that the pain was worth it and that I would learn to swim in the turbulent waters.

And He also knew my enemy could not.

So I smile by the shore gazing out at the water that tried to drown me. Silly waves, you made a warrior!

August 23rd, 2018

"The best worst-case scenario..."

This saying came to mind the other day while visiting with family.

My family, like many of yours, has had a rough year.

I say that because in one week alone, 11 friends on social media posted about a loved one's passing. That's 11 in a single week.

I think about Carmen's passing every single day. I think of the sounds and the smells but, most importantly, I also think of the peace.

I think of getting to plan to some degree how I wanted that moment to be when she slipped from my arms into the Lord's. I think of the days when my family and community carried me without even knowing it. I think of the meals that were brought to our home because I couldn't cook and didn't want to eat. I think of the inspirational cards and gifts that we clung to. I think of the gas cards and the gift cards to Panera that allowed me to get to the hospital fast to just be with my baby.

I think of our mothers who cared for Holland so intently, erasing every other task so that I could be with Carmen. I think of my husband who just started a new job and needed to work so that we could have insurance. I think of the prayers and the words shared with me as I sat alone in a hospital room — prayers and words that echoed in my mind and resounded in Carmen's body.

I think of the money that was given so that we didn't have to worry when the bills came in. I think of the friends that would text me at midnight because I was on their mind and they knew I was up. I think of the gift baskets that were dropped off on my doorstep that were colorful and contained joy and love — baskets that were filled with gifts not only for me but also for Holland, who most days had to learn to be quietly independent. I think of all these things and smile.

I think of the friends who planned Carmen's celebration of life service in detail. The friends who made that day so special that it is raved about even a month later. A day that was so full of life that several times I even forgot that I was at my own daughter's funeral.

I think of the gifts made and given in Carmen's honor:
- A tree to plant.
- A stuffed animal made from her clothing.
- A necklace with her initial.
- Artwork of verses that are dear to my heart.
- A star named after Carmen!

I think of the fact that every single day I got to spend with Carmen was because of others. It wasn't just me.

I think of how blessed, and even more humble, I am now because I learned to accept help. I came to realize that I couldn't rely upon just my own strength to do everything that needs to be done in the midst of life's often-unpredictable circumstances.

I learned that God uses people in truly profound and powerful ways! I think how each moment I got to spend with my special baby girl is because of others. And it breaks my heart because I see those who don't have this. I see mothers whose husbands left when the diagnosis was too much. I see them scrape together their finances, the lack of support, and their efforts to be in three places at once. I see the mothers who are working so hard at their livelihoods but also have what amounts to full-time jobs in just keeping their minds straight and tending to their children that they love equally, though they often feel as if they will never be able to prove it.

I see families struggling, sometimes forced to sell all they have, to help preserve their child's life. I see children suffer and get left behind because the world is broken and it is so easy to give up.

I see eyes full of grief, guilt, and loss. I see arms that have tried to carry the weight of an unrelenting situation that eventually broke and crash-landed them into a life they never could have imagined or intended to be a part of.

I see brokenness like never before and I have a great desire to share all that others did for me and my family because they were used by God to enable us to persevere. We did not fail. We are not broken.

Be blessed in order to be a blessing.

September 6th, 2018

Sunday night as I sat on our couch thinking about this morning's sermon on the subject of sacrifice, I felt a bit stupid, perhaps ignorant, or just plain wrong.

Sacrifice is a word that stings me. It's a word I can feel when it's spoken and yet in some ways I don't feel as if I fully grasp it. I asked myself a few times in the coming week, "I wonder if this is how God felt?" Perhaps that sheds light on why I felt the way I did that Sunday evening. Who on earth can know how God feels?

Did God grieve when He sent His one and only Son to die as the perfect sacrifice for our sins? Did He feel that He sacrificed anything at all?

I don't think God smiled as Jesus was mocked and beaten and killed. I don't think He enjoyed any part of Jesus' suffering. God knew that this world was never going to be Jesus' home. He knew that a sacrifice was necessary. Since He knew the plan He had put into place, which was for Jesus to do for us what we cannot do for ourselves and then return to heaven as ruling King and Lord, the Father didn't grieve how we are inclined to. Jesus was coming home!

When Carmen's days here were coming to an end, everything came into focus. Every single thing she had endured was not to bring joy to God, but it was for a purpose that transcends just this world. It was for the next. And it was necessary. And honestly, I have many days where all I can do is celebrate her being in heaven.

Please know I am by no means comparing my daughter to Jesus. I am only pondering the idea of sacrificing my own love for this world — the life I had thought I would lead, the person I was and thought I would be — for something more; something that, when I think about it, isn't much of a sacrifice at all. Sacrifice in this world is necessary and do so for God leads to gains that are beyond anything this world can provide. In comparison, having "lost" my daughter (one of my most precious ties to this life) has allowed me to have eyes and a heart for others and for eternity.

I am now filled with joy as God has allowed me to see the fruit of Carmen's life and death and is enabling me to better focus on my role advancing His kingdom during my short time here on this planet.

"Do not store up for yourselves treasures on earth…store up for yourselves treasures in heaven …" (Matthew 6:19–20)

September 14th, 2018

I have been dreading today — Holland's two-and-a-half-year check up. She talks about doctors all day long and her sister being at the doctor's office in the sky. She recognizes waiting rooms in businesses and asks where Carmen is. It hurts but in some ways it's nice. I love hearing Carmen's name. I love that Holland remembers her, but I regret some of the memories she has of her.

I hate that Holland looked at me this morning horrified that if she went to the doctors she, too, would not come home again.

September 16th, 2018

It's a dance — beautiful and exhausting.

Sometimes I start off too fast and other times I can't keep up with the music.

They dance with me. We each have our own music.

I try to match my moves with theirs. We have the same moves but we are almost never in sync.

Some days I lead and they follow. Other days I hide in the back, as I forget the next step.

I copy their moves, embarrassed, but I am not allowed to sit down. I don't want to dance this dance anymore. Not like this.

But I must. We must.

My mind can see it come together as my body is aching to stop. I remind myself to breathe, to count, and to pick up where I left off.

This dance is our own — beautiful and exhausting.

It's the dance of grief.

This week was exhausting, both mentally and emotionally. God spoke to me so often and so clearly, and I can truly say that what He has allowed me to see and be part of is humbling. God is great in every sense of greatness one can imagine.

This week I've had questions thrown at me that have made me see the beauty behind many days I thought were only advancements by Satan.

God allowed me to see why I had to have surgery to remove my appendix while pregnant with Carmen. He allowed me to see why her time at home was so short. He allowed me to see why my grandfather passed just months prior to Carmen and He allowed me to see why I stood up there (by myself, mind you) in April and sang at his funeral in front of 500 people.

Singing that day was one of the most indescribable moments I have experienced. I knew I was singing for my granddad and I knew that something would indeed go wrong to the point I would have to sing all alone with no accompaniment. I knew that it would be pleasing to both him and my Lord for me to sing that day. I also knew I was singing for Carmen. I actually pictured myself singing at her funeral even though she was still very much alive. I knew I was singing for every single day of my life.

This week, God impressed upon me that the only thing I would regret if I passed at this very moment is that I didn't worship Him enough. I told God, "But I do sing." And He said, "No, louder!"

It's not just singing He is referring to. We are created to worship. And we all worship something or someone, or even ourselves. I don't want to be just a church singer, or a funeral singer. In fact, I don't want to be a singer at all. I just want to worship God all day long.

Carmen's name meaning "song" has me constantly hearing, "You can't tell her story without it being a song." To me it means that Carmen came to show us how to worship. She taught us to rejoice and to truly sing and dance and celebrate when all we want to do is fall apart.

September 18th, 2018

I truly don't live under the naïve assumption that there are those that have perfect lives, that others are better off than me, or that some people live life without heartache. I honestly have yet to meet someone that I would trade lives with.

I don't envy most and even though my life has not been easy, I haven't met someone who's life has been devoid of serious challenges. We all have things to deal with. Mine are only mine; they are just different than yours. Not necessarily that much harder or any easier.

I have been asked questions such as:

- "Do you think it would have been better if you hadn't met her?"
- "Don't you think it was easier because you had time to prepare?"
- "Wouldn't it be harder without Holland?"
- "Could you imagine if it were sooner/later?"

The answer to all of these questions is yes and no. But it doesn't change anything.

Every single one of us walks around adorned with various chains of hurt, defeat, and things beyond our control that can produce anger, resentment, and jealousy. These chains are used to pull us in certain directions; they shape our eyes, minds, and hearts. Sometimes the chains are visible, at other times they aren't. But we all have them.

What we choose to do with these chains is up to us. We can shrink down and become overpowered, immobilized, and invisible, or we can carry them proudly each day, strengthening our core. That way we are not being defined by the chains but putting them to use by showing others how they can be managed, both gracefully and with power.

The chains never leave. For even in perfect freedom they will remain as the strings of stories and the ribbons of honor showing where we've been and how far we've come.

My chains are mine — sturdy and gold-plated. Some days they wear me down and threaten to immobilize me, but then God steps in and uses them to give me direction, mission, and even affirmation. He grants me His eyes to see just how I should *want* to carry these chains; how I *can* carry them.

Today I love these chains. These chains are strong and I have great power because of them. The glory is all yours, Jesus.

September 20th, 2018

"Please, Mommy! Please, can I see baby Carmen now? Please?"

Holland was convinced that saying the magic word would make it a done deal. I wish I could have said, "Sure, let's go see her right now." Instead of reacting in a fit resentment over having to deal with this heaviness right now, I realized that this was my opportunity to tell her the truth.

So I pulled the car over and said, "Holland, we can't see Carmen anymore. We can see her pictures but we won't see her anymore from where we are." She pointed out the window and said, "She lives over there?"

"No sweetie, Carmen was too sick to live where we live now. She had to go far away to be with God in heaven."
She smiled and said, "No, Mommy! Carmen is not sick. She is so happy!"
"Yes, baby, she is so happy now and one day in a long time, we can all see her again!"
"Can MiMi see her? And Daddy and JoJo and Toby and Luke? And Pete, the cat?"
"Holland I think Pete the cat will have to stay here but one day we can all see Carmen again if we know God."
"Can I push her in the stroller there?"
"Maybe. I think she would love that."
"Okay Mommy. Baby Carmen is so happy! Can I see her butterfly bush?"
"Yes, Holland. Let's go see her butterfly bush."
"I'm not scared Mommy."
"Okay, Holland."

"Carmen's not scared, Mommy."
"I know, baby."

Thank you, God, for allowing me to have this conversation with Holland today. Would I have ever thought to pull the car over and tell my two-and-a-half-year-old of your plan for us if not for Carmen? Not likely.

September 21st, 2018

They say the journey is the best part, even better than the destination. They say getting there is half the fun. The ending of a book is far less meaningful if we just skip to the last page. But I feel like that's what we got.

For some of us, it's as if our plane never left the tarmac or had to turn around just after going wheels up but well before reaching cruising altitude. Even worse are when life circumstances are so dysfunctional that it's as if the airliner crashed less than halfway through the flight.

Excited to go on our long-planned road trip we turn on the radio only to hear the first three notes of a song before the car goes completely out of control. Now not only is the trip over before it even really got started, but we'll never know what song that was!

We were gifted a book that was nicely titled and from afar looked to be hundreds of pages long, but as we got closer and finally opened it up, the only text was "The End" in big, bold letters.

You would think these short-circuited journeys with unknown songs and single-paged books would be easy to forget. Truth is, they are not. These moments, however brief, will at times follow us, other times lead us, and sometimes threaten to consume us. We wanted them to be more. We wanted them to be what they were supposed to be.

We cannot simply pretend to have never bought that plane ticket; we can never stop hearing those first three notes without wondering what song it was. And we can never stop reading that one-paged book. The reason is quite simply that it's what we have; it's our story.

For us the journey isn't the best part as the destination was never the "there" we expected and "The End" was never supposed to come this soon.

September 21st, 2018

I think of holding her again.

But as I think of her death, I was stunned by what actually took place. It was the very last time I would ever hold her and, because of her horrific state, it was the first and last time I had held her in a five-day span.

Her passing took about an hour. It was a struggle for us both. I didn't want to look at her. I just wanted to feel her. I didn't want anyone to have to tell me that she was gone. I wanted to just know myself.

The monitor's sound was turned off in our room. Only the doctors in the hall could hear the noise of a body failing.

She fought and I fought. We both had moments of tenseness and others of complete surrender. In some ways my body was excited, which I assumed was because it didn't know how to react to this kind of experience. There were intermittent times of butterflies followed by throbbing pain; the anticipation felt as if it were killing us both. Adrenalin enabled me to keep from dropping her in spite of being utterly exhausted.

My body started bleeding. It wasn't that time of the month, but maybe that was just one way my body was coping with the loss. It felt natural, in a way, that I would bleed. I didn't care. It felt like it was the last thing I could physically do to let her go. So I just sat there with my eyes closed, bleeding and pleading to God that He would somehow cover us both in peace.

I became almost overwhelmed by the thought that I was actually killing my daughter. This is a thought that threatens to haunt me for the rest of my life. I did not kill my daughter! Quite to the contrary, but in that moment the thought took hold.

Carmen had been marked as DNR (do not resuscitate) for nearly 24 hours. For us, she had already passed. She wasn't our Carmen anymore. And the fact was she was now at the point where attempting to resuscitate her would have brought on even more unnecessary pain and suffering.

It is as if we had been placed in a box that was pitch black. She had to go. It was time. I wanted to hold her the entire time. No matter how scary and no matter the outcome. I needed to hold her all the way until the end. I needed to feel her leave me. It was the only way I was going to believe it.

Once she passed, I had a rush of relief which didn't make sense because all I wanted to do was throw up. My baby girl had just died in my arms. The brokenness covered me. I assumed my heart would stop as well.

Nate wanted to hold her one last time as I wrote my final letter to Carmen. I wanted to write in that air — the atmosphere of death. It was all I had left of her. I hated that day but it was so filled with the power of God, the power of love, and it was a battle Nate and I had watched and participated in. I never want to forget it.

And then I didn't want to hold her anymore. Not because I was scared or didn't miss her right away, but calmness filled us. Carmen wasn't there anymore.

The nurses asked if we wanted to bathe her, wanted more time with her, wanted her fingerprints, an autopsy, or anything at all. We peacefully and confidently said, "No."

It amazes me to visualize myself walking out of that room with her still laying in that bed. How did I do that?

Why didn't I hold her longer? Shouldn't someone have had to come pry her from my arms? Nate pushed our empty stroller and car seat out into the hall. I carried nothing. I didn't want to carry anything anymore.

September 23rd, 2018

This weekend brought me great comfort to know that even Jesus wept. I had been thinking that by not having my life in perfect and deliriously happy harmony, that I would be portraying that I didn't trust God fully, that I lacked faith in His ultimate plan, and/or that I would seem less than what He wanted me to be.

The voice of doubt grew stronger saying things such as:

- *"You wouldn't have taken care of her properly!"* (When I thought about her conditions.)
- *"You knew your body wasn't healthy enough to create a healthy baby!"* (When struggling physically.)
- *"You couldn't have taken care of Holland well enough!"* (When asked if she is my only child.)
- *"You didn't have enough faith to save her, you didn't pray the right way, and you didn't try hard enough!"* (When I was entering the presence of the Lord.)

I was thinking this was God's voice. I began to struggle with the notion that because I couldn't save my daughter, maybe He couldn't save me.

This weekend I was reminded exactly whose voice that was. God never said any of those things! I was reminded that my prayers were heard and answered in the way God saw fit, which is the most perfect, magnificent, and glorifying way. I was reminded of the new eyes God gave me as He took me on this journey. I

331

was reminded that I am redeemed, I am enough, and I am loved.

The voice I was listening to was that bellowing from the remnants of my old, sinful self. The fact that I was choosing to hear that voice as it got increasingly louder and that I let it drive me to fear and despondency is what I needed to be freed from.

One thing's for sure about this road and it's that I am not alone. Maybe that's what has shocked me the most. There are vast numbers of us grieving and traumatized, weary and doubting, and listening to the wrong voice. It doesn't even look like sin. It's masked in emotions and what seem to be completely justified reasons to feel pain. However, make no mistake that this voice is that of a liar.

I let that voice take the place of God's voice. I let that voice convince me I failed. I let that voice fill me with bitterness and I let that voice try and put blinders on the new eyes God had given me. I let that voice tell me His glory wasn't worth it.

September 24th, 2018

Things to keep in mind when a loved one is grieving:

1) How many times a day do you think about your kids? How many times do you talk to others about them? How many times after your children fall asleep do you sit up for an extra 45 minutes and look at their pictures because, as exhausted as you are, for some reason you already miss them?

The answer to these questions is somewhere between frequently and always, right? For those of us who are grieving, this is still the same. We think about them so much. We want to talk about them; we forever miss them.

2) It's okay to bring them up to us; it's okay to say their names. We so badly want you to say their names. We want to know that the whole world didn't forget about them.

3) You may feel uncomfortable but trust me, we *always* feel uncomfortable. You will not remind us of something that we aren't already playing on a repeat loop. You aren't going to be uncomfortable forever, but for a moment you can help us feel human again.

4) The death of a child doesn't only affect the mom. The death of a child throws off the natural rhythm of the world for the entire family unit. It impacts marriages and siblings, grandparents, great-grandparents, and even friends. Please, when you ask how Mom is doing, don't forget the rest of the family, too. Maybe encourage your husband to speak to other husbands who

have had to say goodbye so soon. I know my husband's heart leaps a thousand feet when his baby girl is remembered.

5) Be sensitive to how and why we ask such common yet personal questions. And if we do ask, let's be ready to receive an answer that isn't quite so common but more personal. Never assume you know anything about the mom in front of you.

RANT: While Carmen was in the midst of her 194-day hospital stay I had very few times where I would be able to take my two-year-old for an outing in the attempt to experience simply being normal, whatever that was supposed to mean. I once took her to a spring event where she was having so much fun in a playhouse. I was being so silly with her and just wanted to have a great time because I knew it would be a while before we would have one-on-one time again. While playing, another mom who had about three or four kids looked at me and said, "You are so lucky you only have one to focus on." I almost threw up in my mouth. From the outside, sure, I looked like a carefree mom with one happy toddler. On the inside I was awaiting a phone call from the hospital that my baby's time had come.

6) Think of how you would feel if someone asks when you're going to start a family if in fact you had but then things changed dramatically. Think of how you might stumble when someone asks how many children you have, if the child with you is your only one, or why you wouldn't want her to have a sibling when the plan you had was suddenly and irrevocably altered.

7) Be careful when you try to tell a grieving parent to be thankful for the children they already have. Trust me when I tell you that we are beyond thankful. We value them as complete miracles that honestly baffle us to have at this point. We are honored to be parents more than ever before. Think how you might feel if someone told you to be grateful for your other children. Which one would you give up?

8) Remember that we now have a persistent concern, approaching actual fear, since we have seen death and how easily it comes. We fear losing our other children and the ones we may pray for in the future. Be sensitive if we hesitate to fully embrace certain activities or may seem overprotective for a stage or two.

9) Having another child may seem like an "easy fix" but know that there is not a grieving parent out there who decides to have another child as merely a replacement for the one that was lost. We are talking about humans here, not our favorite pair of shoes.

10) Remember their child at momentous occasions and the in-between times. On holidays or whenever you feel led, send a text, a letter, or a gift to the family.

I have jewelry with Carmen's ashes in them, pictures, statues, and memory boxes. I have a stepping-stone, a comfort tree, and even a star named after her. These things have all helped me to feel connected to her in some way. These things are all we have now. I know they are just things, but they help.

11) Don't give up on us! We are broken and changing. We will never be the same. You can't fix us. We won't get over it and we won't forget our children. Please show us grace and mercy. Don't leave us. Even if we shove the world out, keep loving us. We need it now more than ever.

September 25th, 2018

I've been thinking about the hospital a lot lately. I know it's strange but I miss it. It was Carmen's home for most of her life. I assume that's why I have missed this place so much.

But honestly, I miss who I was there and who I became. Within those walls I found my voice, my heart, and learned much about medicine, the human body, and the power of never quitting.

I learned to fight. I learned that I mattered. I learned that value is sometimes given and sometimes earned. I learned to create and I learned to be completely happy without any change in circumstance. I learned to be brave and strong and articulate. I learned just how small I was and how big I could be.

I learned who I always wanted to be.

September 27th, 2018

All of it! I used to fear it all, because with you everything was so uncertain.

Now I fear because no matter what, it is certain we are apart for the rest of our lives.

October 1st, 2018

You know when you have planned and worked very hard for that special vacation? Imagine getting so close to the end of your "to-do" list before you can leave on your fabulous trip. Oh, the anticipation!

All of the people you love will be there and you are so excited for what you will see and do in this new place. It's going to be great! That list is all that stands in the way of your departure. You know what you have to get done to be able to relax and really enjoy your holiday.

I imagine that's how heaven will be. We all have a "to-do" list to accomplish before we get to go and God is the only one who knows what our particular tasks are.

When Carmen was passing, I saw all the extra work she was putting in. And when she was unable to do anymore, her purpose became clear as day. My goodness was she an overachiever!

When I saw this picture, I saw Carmen there. It made me think of when I have finally checked off all the boxes on my list and I get to go. She, as the perfectly whole person she was created to be, will greet me joyously. It's going to be so wonderful!

October 3rd, 2018

Because October is Pregnancy and Infant Loss Awareness Month, I have been thinking about what best to convey in helping raise awareness for the large community of those facing life having lost a child.

What is loss? Some synonyms are: mislaying, misplacement, forgetting. When I thought more about these words it began to anger me. Think of how these words are often used:

- "I lost my keys."
- "I misplaced my wallet."
- "I forgot where my purse is."

Of all the words used to reference a loved one's death, this has been the most hurtful to me. The simple reason is that "loss" is not what I feel. I didn't mislay my daughter. I didn't misplace her. I didn't forget her.

And neither did God.

This word spells out defeat to me. It's the opposite of a win. This word signifies that some sort of mistake took place when my daughter left my arms and entered the beautiful gates of heaven to be in the very presence of the Lord.

This word allows doubt to enter the minds of mothers whose arms are empty. It's a doubt that can create a false reality that we did something wrong, that maybe our bodies failed to remember what they were supposed to do, that instead of paying attention and holding on to this most precious gift we simply misplaced it.

It leads to the lie that God forgot about our child; the child that was supposed to live, grow, and be here with us. It screams the lie that we do not know where our children are.

When I think about loss awareness, I think about the lost. I think about those who do not have the secure hope in Jesus Christ of an ultimate destination in heaven for all eternity. When I think about loss awareness I think of a mighty God who had an impeccable plan that included our children's end of life. Not because He forgot about them, but because He wanted them for something much more profound.

When I think about the empty wombs, the empty arms, and the empty cribs I think of the empty tomb. I think of the sacrifice that God made when He sent His only Son to walk the earth for a short time with the plan of dying and conquering death in order to make heaven possible for us all.

When I think of our broken hearts, I think of our loving, merciful God who broke my heart to give me a new one—a heart for those I would have never seen without my fractured one.

When I think of our lives as now always "missing" someone, I think of all God's people who are now found because of a life we believed was gone too soon. It hurts deeply, it hurts constantly, and it hurts completely. But it is not a loss!

Over 900 people came to my daughter's funeral. Several hundred watched online. Still today strangers approach me and ask if I am Carmen's mother. And rarely do they depart without telling me that they or someone they know has made or is moving toward making peace with God because of what they saw and heard.

I am not being insensitive when I say this, but today I want to celebrate just as Carmen taught me. I want to celebrate every baby who has been called "lost."

Carmen taught me to celebrate in the midst of pain, anger, and despair. She taught me to sing no matter what. After all, recall that her name means "song" in Latin. Carmen taught me to keep looking up and always know where I came from and where I am going. Never, ever lost. So today we will do what the found do, which is sing, rejoice, and celebrate.

Father God,

Thank you for each child you have entrusted to us. No matter the days, all you ask of us is to love one another. I pray that today we experience and stand firm in the love you have for us and for our children, both near and far. I pray that when darkness surrounds us we can break through with love, peace, and the hope of heaven. I pray that you will continue to allow your light to shine brightly so that we rest assured that your plan is perfect and we are never, ever lost.

Amen

October 4th, 2018

Joy is an inner contentment that remains radiant regardless of the circumstances. It is one assurance that the Lord dwells within us. If we lose our joy we lose our strength.

Because of your life, Carmen Grace, my joy is here to stay.

And we will forever and always be...

Letters

Dear Reader,

I don't know why you chose to read this book but for many reasons I want to say I am sorry.

I wanted to write a great book of the miracle that was Carmen's life. I wanted her to be the success that no one could doubt; that God was within her. I wanted her to be the one to perplex us all and one from whom joy flowed.

I decided to continue to write because Carmen is all of those things to me. I pray that you were able to see those many blessings throughout these pages.

I am sorry because if you are reading this book, you are most likely looking for a miracle. You have, like me, prayed, wished, and are doing all that you can to be the difference-maker. You are forced to fight like never before, even if the first step was opening this book.

Carmen taught me to celebrate every single moment like it was the last, and then she put all my celebrating to the test when I was asked to surrender her to the Lord and celebrate even harder.

Today, with empty arms, I am still celebrating. I am celebrating by telling her story. I am celebrating by loving others in a way I never could before her life. I am celebrating by giving gifts to parents in hospitals — gifts that I hope will help them be able to celebrate. I am celebrating by attempting to change the view of pain, the view of worth, the view of life, and the view of death.

Do not wait for the perfect day. A perfect day does not exist. You can love and celebrate and sing and cry and hope all at the same time.

I wrote this book because today I am jealous to have this book. I am jealous to hold it, to have lived it. I cannot imagine my life without it; every single bit of it.

Today is a good day for a good day. I hope you make it beautiful.

Love,

Sydney & Carmen

Dr. Thompson,

I have wanted to reach out to you, but I haven't known what to say. I think the only thing I can say is, thank you.

Thank you for all that you did to give Carmen the best chance at life. Thank you for always thinking outside the box and taking risks with her when others thought she was too fragile. Thank you for always stopping by and explaining the many things I couldn't understand. Thank you for always reminding me that it is okay to smile.

And as much as I hated that day, I want to thank you for coming to talk to us when it was time to let Carmen go.
If anyone else had come in that room to tell us that, we wouldn't have listened.

I knew with my whole heart that if there were a hint of a chance that Carmen would see the world again, you would have given her that opportunity. I want to thank you for your honesty and compassion.

We love you so much and we know Carmen's story isn't over. I would love to help in the PICU in any way that I can. If there is ever anything my family or I can do, please let us know.

I haven't stopped smiling and I don't plan to.

Thank you again.

Dr. Collazo and Dr. Shelly,

I remember meeting you one cold day in December in a small NICU waiting room. I was absolutely terrified and all I could do was try not to cry. The first few meetings we had, I can honestly say that I had no idea what you were talking about. It was as if I would go deaf when you spoke and I just sat there waiting to disintegrate into the ground.

Fast forward to summer. I am fairly positive I would be able to explain each of Carmen's heart surgeries in detail using correct medical terminology with a smile on my face.

Between then and now, you were there. You protected Carmen and gave her a shot over and over again. Even when you wouldn't be the one working on her, you advocated as if she were yours. I can never thank you enough for that. To me, you were like her great aunt and uncle. You saw her as she was and what she could be. You knew my heart for giving her a beautiful life and you held me accountable and challenged me to be the very best mommy to Carmen.

I know you held back when the news was just too much and you allowed me to experience things as they came. In the beginning I hated this, but I came to realize that each day has enough worries and it is pointless to worry about tomorrow.

I hope you know that I am so grateful for all the work you put into helping Carmen thrive. There is no doubt in my mind that Carmen would have walked and talked and even ran and sang. I am absolutely convinced that she looked forward to the day she could hug you and thank you herself for believing in her.

Thank you for saving Carmen's life. It was short but it was enough and it was absolutely beautiful.

Nurse Kristen,

The day Carmen was discharged from the NICU and admitted to the PICU, you were there. She was grayish-purple and desaturating into the 30s. I stood in the back without an idea of what that meant or what to do. You ripped off your jacket and ran in to administer oxygen to her. She wasn't even your patient and you saved her life.

You took care of Carmen many times but you also took care of me. One night after being at the hospital for 16 hours, I received more bad news and collapsed. You and Brittney saved my life, too. It was a dark time for all of us and even though I want to forget that memory, I will never forget how you helped me.

I loved when you had Carmen. I knew you were quick to act and didn't let things slide. You were never afraid to question the doctors and you always advocated for her. I know you do this for all your patients.

I remember at first thinking that you were a bit stern, but very quickly came to realize and appreciate your manner. You knew exactly what effect you had on that unit and you used all of your power to get children from point A to point B as efficiently as possible. You were a force and you didn't waste time with things that didn't matter.

As time passed, you changed Carmen. I will take a risk and say I think Carmen changed you as well. I think she showed you that life in the PICU was still life and that the smaller, perhaps less significant details, were still important. I think she showed you that you could save lives without administering oxygen. You could save lives by creating it. Life is breath and light and hope all wrapped into a moment and each one is just as important as the next.

By spring you were secretly singing to Carmen, getting her dressed up and even playing with her! I knew you were sold and it made me so happy that my little girl was safe and loved by you.

On the last night of Carmen's short life, you helped me to sleep next to her in a big bed. You gave me precious moments that no one else could. You also expressed a desire to become a nurse practitioner and I know you will be terrific in that role. My family and I would like to help you be able to do that. We would like you to accept a scholarship from Carmen to help you on your way to becoming an NP! We would be honored to help you in any way we are able as you embark on this journey.

Thank you, Kristen.

Dearest friend Nancy,

There are few things in life that are so clearly examples of God's finest work that it almost makes you want to burst out in joyous laughter. One of those works is you! God placed you in Carmen's life because He knew we all needed you. He used you to bring comfort and understanding to my family and me as we walked through a brand new calling. You gave compassion and a sense of realness to a grueling situation and you exhibited genuine grace because you too have experienced the loss of a child.

You helped me navigate the hospital and constantly reminded me *Who* we belong to. You fought the battle alongside us with tear-filled eyes. You never, ever gave up. You know the power of Jesus and you expect to see His work every single day.

You taught me to look for Him in all things and you taught me to use what I am going through to bless other people. You taught me to turn confusion, anger, and despair into hope, joy, and peace. You saw the challenges and knew full well the dark road Carmen walked, but you always found the light. And when there was no light left, you became a source of light.

I know you cared for Carmen in a special way. I know God laid her name on your heart for a reason. I believe that through the care you gave Carmen, you honored the life of your son who is now in heaven. Bobby's story continued through you and through Carmen. And now I will carry Carmen's story with me in all I do and I pray that I can bless someone else one day just as magnificently as you have blessed me.

I love you, Nancy.

To the amazing INOVA Fairfax PICU team,

Carmen Hatcher was blessed to meet so many of you throughout her six-and-a-half-month stay. Some of you spent months beside her and others just a few hours. Each and every one of made quite an impact.

My prayer for Carmen was always that she would come home. And she did! I never said for how long.

Each of you played a significant role in making this a reality. Many of you assisted in making Carmen's life in the hospital as beautiful as it could be!

It has been a very difficult year but I wanted to tell you all that I know Carmen was exactly where she needed to be for just the right amount of time. I know that you all did everything you could to extend her life and make it full and for that I am exceedingly grateful! You all did an incredible job and never once did you give up on her.

I hope that Carmen's long stay in the PICU gave you a glimpse at just how important you are. You helped her endure and recover after numerous surgeries that often included setbacks. It was hard work, but she was able to do it with your care!

The work was not in vain. Carmen's life changed hundreds of lives and I will always do my best to make sure her story lives on. One of the ways I hope to accomplish this is by publishing her story. I wrote most every day while Carmen was in the hospital and each day when she came home, up until now.

The writings are raw and real; my soul has been poured in these words. My hope is that it could be a resource for other parents who receive a challenging pre- or postnatal diagnosis.

I did my best to celebrate Carmen's victories, both big and small, and my hope is that this book inspires other parents having to do life in the hospital to find the strength to celebrate each day.

I love you all and I will certainly be visiting as often as I feel led.

Each and every one of you will remain in my thoughts and in my heart forever.

For each book purchased, *Carmen's Miracle Makers* receives a donation!

Carmen's Miracle Makers strives to inspire and equip parents of critically ill children with tools to encourage bonding and memory-making while enduring a lengthy PICU stay.

Thank you for assisting us in helping another family celebrate today!

www.carmensmiraclemakers.org

40815915R00203

Made in the USA
Middletown, DE
31 March 2019